W9-ATR-555

Arnulfo L. Oliveira Memorial Library

THE
DRUM
BOOK

GEOFF NICHOLLS

The Drum Book
A history of the rock drum kit
By Geoff Nicholls

Published in the UK by Balafon Books, an imprint of Outline Press Ltd,
115J Cleveland Street, London W1P 5PN, England.

Published in the United States by Miller Freeman Books
600 Harrison Street, San Francisco, CA 94107
Publishers of *Guitar Player* and *Bass Player* magazines
Miller Freeman, Inc. is a United News and Media company

un Miller Freeman
A United News & Media company

ISBN 0-87930-476-6

Printed in Hong Kong

Art Director: Nigel Osborne
Design: Sally Stockwell
Photography: Miki Slingsby
Editor: Tony Bacon

Typesetting by Type Technique, London
Print and origination by Regent Publishing Services
97 98 99 00 01 5 4 3 2 1

C O N T E N T S

INTRODUCTION

This is the first book to describe the development of the rock drum kit in relation to players and musical movements. The Drum Book is the story of the drums, of the manufacturers, and of the players whose needs fuelled the changes.

Although rock music really got going in the 1950s, the drum kit had been around since early in the 20th century, and the modern drum kit had already taken shape in the late 1930s. So when rock'n'roll was born the drum kit was simply adopted by the new rock drummers. And when Ringo Starr proudly played his Ludwig kit on American TV in 1964 the floodgates were opened.

Rock got louder and heavier, and drum kits were strengthened and enlarged, reaching a peak with the massive 'stadium-rock' kits of the 1980s. The Japanese makers revolutionised the scene, while more recently the American and European drum manufacturers have again revitalised the market. American, Oriental and European drums compete today on their own terms for a share of the international market.

My aim with this book has been to include as much as possible while keeping the whole readable and enjoyable. It is a personal interpretation of what happened, from a British perspective, built largely on a crop of specially conducted interviews with some of the men who were actually there. You'll also find an unrivalled gallery of specially commissioned photographs of rare and beautiful drums, and towards the back a directory with more information on individual makers. I've attempted throughout to relate the story of the equipment to the changes that took place in rock music, and in doing so I hope we don't lose touch with the fact that the drums were made in the first place to be played.

GEOFF NICHOLLS, ENGLAND, FEBRUARY 1997

"I thought – they've got such a unique sound, so why clutter it up?"
DJ Fontana EXPRESSES HIS DOUBT WHEN ASKED TO ADD DRUMS TO ELVIS PRESLEY'S GUITAR-AND-BASS BAND

"Jerry Allison with Buddy Holly was a schooled drummer and we weren't. Every drummer played 'Peggy Sue' hand to hand, but he played it as a paradiddle. We didn't even know what a paradiddle was."
ADAM FAITH'S DRUMMER **Bob Henrit** ON THE EARLY LOOK-AND-LEARN DAYS OF BRITISH ROCK

"We did Ringo a deal, and then Brian Epstein said, 'Can you get the bass drum head painted for us for TV?'"
BRITISH LUDWIG IMPORTER **Ivor Arbiter** ON THE BIRTH OF THE BEATLES' BASS DRUM LOGO

"I saw Ringo and thought, 'I want to do what he's doing.' I could see a use for the drum lessons I'd been having for the past four years."
FUTURE AMERICAN SESSION DRUMMER **Andy Newmark** IDENTIFIES THE TURNING POINT IN ROCK'N'ROLL DRUMMING

"You don't realise the importance of what you did until later. If I'd have known 1960s music was so important I would have played better."
TOP BRITISH SESSION DRUMMER **Clem Cattini** LOOKS BACK IN WONDER

"When Keith Moon got on the drum kit he played like a maniac. The ironical thing was that it turned out so good."
MOON'S FRIEND **Gerry Evans** UNDERLINES THE FEELING THAT SOMETHING WILD AND PRIMITIVE IS LURKING JUST BENEATH THE DRUMMER'S BEAT

"Highest quality at lowest prices."
EARLY MARKETING PHRASE FROM **Pearl**, AN ORIENTAL COMPANY THAT HAS NOW BECOME THE LARGEST DRUM MANUFACTURER IN THE WORLD

THIS PAGE: Charlie Morgan's Premier Signia Versace kit (left) with custom-made black Paiste Signature cymbals. Now where's that spanner? A selection of calf head logos (above) of varying thickness and quality from Premier's 1939 catalogue.

OPPOSITE PAGE, TOP: The success of the plastic drum heads of Remo Belli (left) eased the way to louder rock drumming styles and the proliferation of rock drummers from the 1960s. William F Ludwig Snr with his brother Theobald began manufacturing under the Ludwig & Ludwig name in 1910, and from 1937 William was joined by his son Bill Ludwig Jnr (left in 1959 colour picture).

OPPOSITE PAGE, MIDDLE ROW: Jay Jones (on the left), a descendant of James P Cooley who with Silas Noble founded the Noble & Cooley company in the 19th century, is pictured with Bob Gatzen, designer of the modern Noble & Cooley drums. Fred Della-Porta (centre), brother of Premier's founder Albert Della-Porta, was responsible for building up Premier's overseas markets in over 100 countries worldwide. Fred is pictured at the Premier factory in 1967 handing over the 'Pictures Of Lily' custom kit to Keith Moon of The Who. Karlheinz Weimer, the man behind Trixon drums, surely the most bizarre designs ever marketed, discusses the new Buddy Rich Luxus metal-shell snare drum with the drumming genius himself (right) way back in 1967.

OPPOSITE PAGE, BOTTOM: The design innovations of George Way (left) grace every modern drum kit. Ivor Arbiter (astride a Hayman drum, right) was the man who gambled on importing expensive Ludwig drums into impoverished Britain in the early 1960s and reaped substantial rewards courtesy of a band called The Beatles.

WHERE MANPOWER is plentiful – in African or Latin music, in the carnivals of Trinidad and Brazil, in the military band and even the symphony orchestra – percussion is a group effort. What's special about the modern drum kit is that one player, incorporating influences from all these areas of music, does everything on his or her own. The drum kit is a percussion section in miniature.

The art of playing the drum kit, which was unknown before the early part of this century, has progressed at a breathtaking rate and remains in constant development today. The drummer's co-ordination of all four limbs has always held a fascination. Through the course of the decades, the reaction of audiences has swayed between awe at the audacious feats of dexterity and a suspicion, aroused by the sometimes tortured physicality of the execution, that something wild and primitive lurks just beneath the beat. Whether drumming is primitive or not, it is certainly ancient. Percussion historian James Blades has cited evidence of percussion instruments dating back 30,000 years. But for now we need only go back to the start of the present century.

Never has the cliché of the cultural melting pot been more apt than in turn-of-the-century New Orleans, where the coming of age of the American nation threw together musical ingredients which would soon excite the whole Western world. The early history of jazz is a complex story which many have tried to penetrate. But whatever the truth, jazz undoubtedly set in motion a musical evolution which led eventually to the greatest popular movement in music: rock'n'roll. And the one instrument which has featured throughout is the drum kit.

The drum kit wasn't invented for jazz, but the extraordinary way jazz focused on rhythm determined the drum kit's development. At the start of the 20th century, drums and cymbals did exist, of course, but they were played as separate instruments, generally while the player was standing up – and in the case of military bands, while marching. In the theatre, restrictions of space and of budget encouraged drummers to play as many instruments as possible. One result was the sleight of technique known as 'double drumming' whereby one drummer played both bass drum and snare drum by hand. Early photos show the snare drum tilted alarmingly close to vertical – which no doubt eased the movement between snare and bass. Drummers could "beat a fast four-in-a-bar bass drum, doing a close roll on snare at the same time" as British drummer Len 'Doc' Hunt once described it.

But the modern drum kit can really be dated from the time when drummers sat down to play the bass drum with a footpedal. This had been tried in the 1890s but was made properly workable by the expeditious tinkerings of William F. Ludwig, an ambitious young Chicago percussionist. The story goes that William, frustrated at not being able to play the fashionable fast ragtime beats, built a footpedal with a spring to return the beater, simultaneously gaining speed and easing the leg-work. This was in 1909. By 1910 he and his brother Theobald, also a percussionist, were in business making pedals for every other drummer around town. With the timely help of sister Elizabeth handling the accounts and her husband Robert Danly (a talented mechanical engineer), the Ludwig name was set to become the most famous in drum kit history.

The practical bass pedal pretty well eliminated the art of double drumming and paved the way for the modern drum kit. The seated drummer could now play both the bass drum and the snare drum with a smile on his face, leaving plenty of energy for the rest of the kit.

CONSOLES, CLANGERS AND TRAPS

After World War I there was an expansion in live music. Large orchestras were employed in hotels and theatres as well as to accompany the silent movies of the day. Drum companies thrived. Ludwig & Ludwig peaked in the mid 1920s, and just survived the great Depression of the 1930s.

Through this period drum kits retained the exaggeratedly large bass drums left over from the marching bands (28″ or more). Everything but the kitchen sink was suspended on and around the bass drum, soon leading to the development of a metal 'console' which surmounted the bass drum and supported 'swan neck' cymbal holders, Chinese toms (with tacked-on and painted non-tuneable heads) and other percussion, plus a swing-out bracket to cradle the snare drum. On top of the console was a 'traps' (contraptions) tray with space for bird whistles, klaxons, ratchets and other sound effects (contemporary catalogues offer dozens of amusing items) plus posts for mounting temple blocks and cowbells.

At this stage cymbals, which were Chinese or, for the more wealthy, 'K' Zildjians imported from Turkey, were mostly small, perhaps 12″ in diameter, and used for effect rather than to carry the rhythm. The concept of playing 'ride' rhythms on cymbal or hi-hat came later (although Baby Dodds, playing with King Oliver's Creole Jazz Band in the 1920s, reputedly had a 16″ Zildjian and may have been the first drummer to play the now familiar jazz ride cymbal beat).

The first intimations of the hi-hat go back to the so-called 'clanger', a small cymbal mounted upright on the bass drum rim and struck by an offshoot arm of the bass pedal (see photograph of the Ludwig pedal on p.11). This was replaced by the 'snow shoe' which comprised two hinged, foot-shaped boards with a pair of cymbals bolted to the ends. This device was placed on the floor and the cymbals clashed together bellows-fashion. Next came the 'low boy' or 'low-hat', similar to the hi-hat but with the cymbals just a few inches off the ground. It took until the late 1920s to do what now seems blindingly obvious: to extend the vertical tube and raise the cymbals so that they could be played by hand as well as foot.

The first hi-hat may well have been fashioned by Barney Walberg of the leading drum accessory company Walberg & Auge around 1926. Certainly Walberg & Auge supplied hi-hats and other items of hardware to most of the drum companies for the next 40 years. Although the hi-hat's inventor is not certain, almost the first and for many still the greatest artist of the hi-hat was Papa Jo Jones, who played with such grace and swing in the Count Basie Orchestra.

AFTER THE DEPRESSION

From the mid 1930s through the war years the inherent swing of American music swept around the Western world and found its principal expression in large dance orchestras. Where jazz in the 1920s had been lively and colourful, swing upped the decibels, and excitable college kids perfected curious jerking dances – 'jitterbugging' – in response to a ferociously swinging beat.

History chose to put Gene Krupa in the spotlight, and for the first time a drummer became an international star. Not only was Krupa young, white and cocky, but his playing was brash, confident, stylish and visual. And his drum kit was overwhelmingly futuristic, all gleaming white pearl – and with none of the novelty sound effects associated with music theatre. Those mainstays of the traps set which are now seen as 'quaint'

– woodblocks, Chinese toms, farmyard noises and the like – were instinctively stripped away by Krupa, leaving behind the basic four-drum configuration now familiar to us all and creating a kit for serious boogie-ing. By one of those fortuitous accidents of history Krupa bypassed the Ludwigs as well as Leedy, the other major name of the era, and had his drums made by Slingerland, a company which hitherto had been on the sidelines but was now elevated to the number one spot.

It's gone down in drumming folklore that the phenomenon of Gene Krupa soloing on his deep tom tom during 'Sing, Sing, Sing' with The Benny Goodman Orchestra from the mid 1930s was *the* major turning point for the drummer in the modern world. The flailing, wild-eyed Krupa launched, for good or bad, the concept of the crowd-rousing drum solo, at the same time achieving the familiarity of a household name and a popularity for a drummer only since overtaken by Ringo Starr.

Of course, Krupa was by no means the first drummer to pound the tom toms. 'Jungle rhythms' were synonymous with early jazz, and the elegant Sonny Greer with Duke Ellington's Orchestra was Krupa's equal as a showman, but Krupa it was who stole the headlines and was regularly seen in the new 'talkie' movies. Moreover, the drum kit as we know it today stems from Krupa's concept. His Slingerland Radio King is the model from which every kit since has followed, recognisable as the same type of instrument you might see any time on MTV (indeed, if retro-fashions continue it may well be the same kit). The lean, four-piece Slingerland Radio King kit of the late 1930s was developed to drive the powerful orchestras of the swing era, through the war years to the end of the 1940s. Thereafter big bands became increasingly uneconomical and jazz went highbrow with bebop, allowing rock'n'roll to take its place as *the* popular music during the 1950s. As we shall see, the drum kit was then gradually adopted and adapted by the developing rock'n'roll drummers.

LUDWIG AND LEEDY

The Ludwig brothers were not the first drum manufacturers in the United States. They actually started out as Chicago agents for the fabulously named Ulysses Grant Leedy, who like them was a percussionist. In 1895 – some 15 years earlier than the Ludwigs – Leedy had decided that if the tools of his trade were to be improved he'd have to do it himself. Leedy drums in

Premier big band kit with Swingster console (front, above; see also main photo, right) Finished in Glitter Gold with green/red Sparkling Brilliant diamonds, the kit has a 28" bass drum plus double-headed 12", 14" and 16" tom toms. The large traps tray has four posts supporting Korean temple blocks. The small Chinese-type tom was made by Premier. The 10x14 snare drum has art deco Dominion Ace single lugs (late 1930s) and dual top and bottom snares. The two smaller tom toms are post-1939, while the larger tom with flat-section rims and collar hooks is from the mid 1930s. The Premier "High Hat" has a brass footplate; but note the mounted, closed hi-hat — now called an X-hat, but seen as early as the 1920s.

10

Sleigh bells (left) Owner Sir Alan Buckley believes these 1920s brass sleigh bells were made by Premier. Drummers were called upon to provide all manner of sound effects for the music theatre and to accompany silent movies. The effects were kept to hand on the "traps" (contraptions) tray and might include bird whistles, klaxons, even animal growls.

12" Cymbal (left) Considered large for the 1920s and early 1930s, it was suspended by curtain cord from "swan-neck" cymbal mounts bolted to the console. Cymbals were generally used for "choked" accents — crashed and then trapped by hand.

Premier Swingster endorsers

(left) Premier's world-beating Swingster Console was named after the 1934 pedal, and produced from 1936. Featured in Premier's 1939 catalogue were two of the foremost British big band drummers, Max Bacon (top) of Ambrose's Orchestra, pictured with the first black and silver Raytex Wonder Finish kit, and Lew Stevenson (centre) of the Jack Hylton Band. (Both their kits have double-headed toms.) The great American swing band leader William "Chick" Webb (bottom) used a Premier Swingster console with his Gretsch Gladstone kit. Webb was famous for his meticulous fills and blurringly fast solos. He was also the first to drop "bombs", syncopated bass drums accents that wouldn't become commonplace until the bebop drummers of the 1940s and 1950s.

Calf head logos

(above) Three batter heads from 1939, the top grade 'signed' by Premier's first production manager, George Smith. Fitting heads was not as simple as today: Premier advised that you lay the shell on paper and draw round it to determine the right size flesh hoop for lapping.

Premier Wonder Finishes 1939

(above) "Sparkling Brilliants" were supplied in Crystal, Gold, Green, Red or Blue with contrasting diamond shapes.

Footpedals

(left and below) The Premier Swingster 282 twin-spring pedal (left) with lambswool beater appeared in 1934. Also English, the wooden-base Windsor pedal (below, left) was made in the 1920s. The two early Ludwig & Ludwig pedals (below) were engineered by Robert Danly from William F Ludwig's 1909 wooden prototype.

various guises continued to be available into the 1950s, but did not quite impact on the rock era. However, Leedy's influence on the evolution of the drum kit is assured thanks to significant contributions such as the first adjustable snare drum stand (1898) and the first pearl coverings (1926) called Pyralins.

Leedy also had an illustrious employee, George Way, whose name every old-drum fan must speak in tones of excited reverence. Way pops up all over the place and is credited with many innovations. One of the most important is his die-cast tension lug with incorporated swivel nut, which we'll come to in a moment.

Way even made it over to Europe in the mid 1920s, promoting Leedy's products and influencing European ideas. An early British customer was Doc Hunt who bought a black and gold Leedy kit from Hawkes of London (later Boosey & Hawkes). Thus inspired, the Doc went on to become a renowned figure in British drum making and renovating, right through the rock revolution. Leedy became a familiar name in the advertisement sections of the British musicians' newspaper *Melody Maker*, while later astute rock drummers from Ginger Baker to Neil Peart have often played Leedy snare drums.

DEFINING THE MODERN KIT

But let's get back to the drum kit's evolution. If you look at the first few picture spreads in this book you'll see that there is a huge leap from the console kits to Slingerland's Radio King, and thereafter a less obvious progression to the kits of the 1960s. To complete the modern kit, several things needed to be in place. These would help to define the present-day drum kit as a bona fide instrument that hasn't changed substantially for half a century.

Some of the ingredients were incorporated before the Radio King, some afterwards. We've seen how the bass drum pedal and hi-hat were invented. Another important pre-Krupa development was the throw-off snare strainer which Robert Danly fashioned for the early pace-setting Ludwig & Ludwig snare drums, around 1914. Before this, apparently the only way to get a tom tom effect on snare drum was to jam a stick between snares and head – which didn't do the snares a lot of good. But what really characterised the Krupa kit is the fact that the traps were jettisoned and the tom toms promoted. The importance that Krupa placed on the tom tom was

demonstrated by the way he asked Slingerland to make his toms tuneable top and bottom – 'double-headed' as we now say. Previously, tom toms which had top skins that you could tune by turning tension bolts still had the bottom skin crudely tacked on. The tom tom had come of age.

Dumping the console and traps was all very well, except that now you had the problem of how to suspend cymbals and toms. The easy solution was simply to clamp items to the bass drum rims. Rim-mount cymbal stands became synonymous with Krupa. Ads in Britain over the next decade referred to 'Krupa American style' kits with 'Krupa style' mounts.

Next, the large tom was sat on a sort of cradle, equivalent to a very low snare drum basket. It was an easy step then to fit legs to the floor tom. As for the smaller tom, the honours go to Scotsman-in-New-York Bill Mather, who devised a shell-mount tom holder based on a short section of the old console. This became known at first as the 'Ray McKinlay model', after another famous drummer of the time, and then as the 'consolette'. The shell-mounted consolette was made by Walberg & Auge for most companies over the next three decades. In fact a mount of the same design, barely updated, was still being fitted to Ludwig's Buddy Rich outfit in 1980.

The other striking aspect of the Radio Kings was the lugs, the metal brackets into which the tension bolts are screwed. Until the mid 1930s most lugs were of a tubular pipe design. Robert Danly, again, had set the pace by fitting tubular lugs to Ludwig's first metal snare drum in 1911. Previously, tension bolts had screwed into simple 'studs' top and bottom which tended to put a strain on the shell. Tubular lugs became the standard through to the introduction of the Radio Kings. In fact the earliest of Slingerland's Radio King toms had short two-point mounted tubular lugs, but they were soon replaced by cigar-shaped Streamlined die-cast lugs, first seen on the Radio King snare drums.

The die-cast lug had actually been introduced previously by George Way when he was working at Leedy. When die-cast lugs were reintroduced they caught on partly because they gave drum companies a strong visual brand identity, but also because they enclose another one of Way's brilliant little ideas – the swivel nut. This vital gadget allows some leeway when lining up the metal rim and the tension rods, greatly easing tensioning and reducing the incidence of threads being stripped. Swivel nuts were soon added to the streamlined lugs, so now tom toms were on a par with bass drum and snare drums in power and tuneability. Cast lugs with swivel nuts have been standard ever since, right up to the reintroduction of tubular pipe lugs during the 1980s in an effort to recreate the classic snares of the 1920s.

The rims (or counter hoops) that these lugs were designed to pull down had also undergone a number of changes. Back in the last century drums generally had wooden hoops and were rope tensioned. The first metal rims were flattened circles of brass or steel which were pulled down onto the 'flesh hoop' of the skin by threaded tension bolts which slotted into clips or claws, sometimes called collar hooks.

These hooks were first used by one Emile Boulanger who founded the Duplex drum company around 1900 and was another pioneer of modern snare drum design. The hooks slipped over the metal rims in the same manner that bass drum claws still do today. Sometimes the tension bolts would be mini timpani style 'T' rods... but you can probably imagine the embarrassment as you launch into your Krupa-style drum feature and your sticks catch under the T rods and fly off, clouting you in the eye. (Similar 'T' rods can be seen on the Carlton kit on p.14/15.) Krupa's early Radio Kings had clips with screw bolts, rather than 'T' rods.

Rims gradually evolved from having a flat cross section to an 'L' cross section with a lower ridge which pushed down onto the flesh hoop of the skin. After this they gained a more substantial ridge through which holes were drilled to thread the tension bolts, what we'd now call a 'double flanged' rim – and another Leedy first.

Characteristic of the style of Krupa and his contemporaries was the use of rim shots. This is where the stick hits both the rim and the head at the same time, giving a loud crack which cuts through the music. Rim shots make for exciting rolls, but unfortunately chew up sticks. And although the Slingerland Radio King rims of flat-section brass were called Stick Savers, this was hardly the truth.

The answer was to turn the top edge of the metal rim over and out in order to save on sticks, a solution hit upon in 1938 by Ludwig's then engineer Cecil Strupe, another venerable name in drum history. Slingerland, incidentally, were very late to embrace this 'triple flange' concept, and when they did –

maybe they were piqued? – their Rim-Shot metal rims had the top lip turned the other way, in other words *in* towards the centre of the drum. Also, Radio King snares were still being offered in 1970s catalogues with original style rims, which must have looked pretty weird to new drummers.

SOLID VERSUS PLY

The metal fittings of a drum are one half of the story. The other half is the shell. In the early 20th century drums were made from solid planks of timber, which were steam-bent and held in the round by 'reinforcing rings' or 'glue rings', hoops of wood glued around the inner top and bottom edges of the shell.

Leedy, for example, made beautiful shells from solid walnut, mahogany and maple. Plywood wasn't in common use until after the mid 1930s. The Radio King snare drums which have been elevated to such a mythic status in recent years were made from solid maple, or occasionally mahogany, about a quarter of an inch thick.

One argument for a solid piece of timber is that you get the distinctive tonal quality of pure wood, uninterrupted by layers of glue. Plywood on the other hand is structurally more stable since the plies are generally glued together with their grains going in opposing directions. The extra stability provided by cross-laminated plies means that the shell is less likely to crack or go out of round. (It's interesting to note that Noble & Cooley today market a *parallel* grain ply line called Horizon, the idea being to emulate solid wood.)

Still, many of today's top recording drummers use restored Radio Kings and other vintage drums in preference to any modern drum. They feel that the tone is better. There are various reasons why this might be so. It's been suggested to me by drum restorer Pat Picton that the timber used in these old drums was of a superior quality, cured for perhaps a couple of years prior to working, and moreover that the wood has since matured with age, like a fine wine. Also, in today's machine-tool age, there are fewer craftsmen experienced at bending a relatively thick plank of hard wood into the round.

Another factor worth considering is that old drums tend to have deeper snare beds than is common today. The snare bed is the groove shaved into the bottom bearing edge on both sides of the shell, around the areas where the snares are attached, designed to give a better snare-to-head contact. Deeper snare

13

12″ Cymbal (left) During the early 20th century cymbals were imported from China, Turkey and Italy. The cruder Chinese types were more common at first, as the Turkish 'K' Zildjians were expensive. Larger cymbals gradually caught on through the 1930s as the jazz pioneers began to incorporate them rhythmically and musically. Chick Webb (see far right) played Zildjians and a large China type during the 1930s.

Carlton kit c1938 (front, above) Everything except the hi-hat is mounted on the console, including the snare drum which has a fold-out bracket. The console could be wheeled on-stage and secured by brakes. The drums here are finished in silver glitter which has turned gold over the years, but Carlton's 1937 catalogue listed an incredible variety of finishes: glitters and pearls, but also Blue Rhapsody, Electra, Waterwave and, best of all, Silver Butterfly Wing.

British sticks c1930s (right) Premier made "black rosewood" sticks in this heavy H model from the same wood the company used for xylophone keys, and pointed out that it was far more durable than ebony. Hickory sticks were more common then, as now.

Carlton kit c1938 (above; see also front, left) This big band kit, with Ridgemount console, is similar to Carlton's Super kit, but assembled from various sources. The two smaller toms have two-point mounted short-tube lugs from around 1936, while the 16″ tom has the art deco bridge lugs fitted from about 1938 until after World War II. All the toms (probably ash) are single-headed, with wooden hoops and timpani 'T' handle tuning bolts. (The 'T' handles have been replaced by screw bolts on the playing side of the large tom to avoid catching sticks.) The bottom heads were tacked on, and varnished to keep out moisture. Hardware includes a Carlton Star twin-post split-heel bass pedal, Carlton Dandy flat-plate hi-hat with tripod legs and deep-cup hi-hats, and an American 1930s Walberg & Auge stool.

Chick Webb (above) The great American swing drummer played Gretsch Gladstone drums with British Premier Swingster consoles. Despite his hunched stature, Webb had enormously strong hands and feet and was arguably the first major jazz drumming virtuoso, famously out-playing Gene Krupa at a 'Battle of the Bands' in 1937.

Carlton Single snare c1937 (left) This modern-looking 6½ x 14 drum has a ply shell with reinforcing hoops, and a 'single' snare of silk wires fitted beneath the bottom head (but not the top head). The same type of three-point snare strainer was exported to America for the Slingerland Radio King. The eight square box lugs were fitted until about 1938 after which art deco-style lugs took over. In 1937 the drum was available in 13 finishes at £36.17s.6d (£36.88, about $60).

Carlton badge (right) Carlton drums were made by John E Dallas & Sons from late 1935 right up to 1968 when they were superseded by Hayman (Dallas-Arbiter). Carlton took their name from the posh Carlton Hotel in central London, while the Ridgemount console was named after the Ridgemount Street address of the Dallas buildings. In the 1930s and 1940s Carlton's competitors included Premier, Ajax and John Grey.

THE CHRONOGICAL
CHICK WEBB
AND HIS ORCHESTRA
1929 - 1934
WITH LOUIS JORDAN, BENNY CARTER, TAFT JORDAN,
JOHN KIRBY, CLAIRE JONES, SANDY WILLIAMS,
ELMER WILLIAMS...
CLASSICS

beds were cut in the days of real animal skins because the natural material would distort to fit the bed without the wrinkling which the more uniform and tougher modern plastic heads display. The deep bed allows the snares to sit flat against the bottom head without them having to be over-tightened with the risk of choking the drum. Hey presto! A crisper sound.

PLAYING PLYWOOD

Today most drums are manufactured from plies of wood. When drum manufacturers went over to plywood they still used glue rings. This was because the plywood was bought ready-laminated and was simply bent and butt-jointed in the same way as if it were a solid piece of timber. So enter another legendary name in American drum history: that of the Fred Gretsch Manufacturing Company of Brooklyn, New York. Gretsch from the 1940s came up with a major modernising concept for the manufacture of ply shells.

Gretsch started to laminate their three-ply shells themselves, offsetting the plies so that the shell is joined in several places instead of just one. This dispensed with the need for glue rings and left straight-walled, unobstructed shells. Gretsch then moved to four plies in the 1950s and finally to six plies in the 1960s, although the thickness of their shells remained roughly the same throughout.

Some people feel this is the optimum shell design: a fairly thin shell, cross-laminated with staggered seams for strength, and without any internal obstructions from glue rings. It may explain why Gretsch have a special place in the history of jazz and rock, with fans ranging from Max Roach and Louie Bellson through to Phil Collins and Vinnie Colaiuta. As with Radio Kings, there are many drummers who may well endorse and play other makes but nonetheless keep a prized Gretsch set at home or for studio work.

There is of course another very persuasive reason for using plywood, which is that it's less expensive. Different types of timber can be used in a single shell. A cheaper wood may be used inside while a special type with an interesting grain may be added to the outside, and another type – perhaps a harder wood – on the inside to increase brightness and projection. Classic Ludwig three-ply shells from the 1950s and 1960s, for instance, used a particular combination of mahogany for the inner and outer plies and then poplar in the middle. Ludwig

would also sometimes opt to use a maple or birds-eye maple outer veneer in order to give a beautiful natural wood finish.

EUROPEAN INTERLUDE

While America was forcing the pace with new music, we must not forget that in Europe, with its immense military and classical traditions, there was also a long history of fine drum manufacturing. Indeed, the brass-shelled drum which inspired William Ludwig to go into the drum making business was German, almost certainly made by Sonor. Dating back to 1875, Sonor is the leading modern German drum company. The market leader in Britain is Premier, founded in 1922 by the Della-Porta brothers, and by the 1930s the major manufacturer of consoles, with booming exports. In fact Chick Webb, one of the greatest American jazz drummers of the day, was featured in early Premier catalogues playing a Gretsch Gladstone kit with a Premier Swingster console. We'll return to the British scene a little later.

THE IMPORTANCE OF SIZE

By the 1950s and the emergence of rock'n'roll the drum kit was virtually settled as an integrated instrument. In its basic format there would be a bass drum, snare drum, one mounted tom tom and one floor tom tom, along with hi-hat, a ride cymbal and a crash cymbal. Usually the ride cymbal and small tom would be mounted on the bass drum. Additionally there would be a bass drum pedal that had a beater faced with lambs wool or leather. A second floor-standing cymbal stand had also been introduced. This was a glorified music stand made from flat strips or tubes of metal with legs which folded out flat, similar to the way microphone stands do today. Finally, there might be a lightweight, collapsible drum stool, although often any available chair or bar stool would have to do.

The sizes of the drums had also been decided. The bass drum had undergone the biggest change. The earliest jazz bass drums had been carried marching drums of large diameter and narrow depth – typically 28x14 or more. Once these were placed on the floor it took until the late 1930s before smaller diameters started to creep in. In Britain, our old friend Doc Hunt was kept busy for a while after World War II cutting down large bass drums to smaller sizes for those drummers who couldn't afford a new drum. A smaller bass drum meant you could mount the newly improved tom toms on top and still have a chance of being seen over the top. However, drummers retained the tendency to sit high, right through to the 1970s.

Eventually the 14x22 bass drum became standard, although some big band players like Buddy Rich favoured a 24″ (and in fact Buddy's final restored Radio King bass drum was a 26″). Bigger bass drums have also been preferred by many recent rockers, including Andy Newmark, who's played with everyone from Sly Stone to Roxy Music, and Led Zeppelin's John Bonham, who played a 26″. The problem with 26″ or larger drums is that the beater strikes the drum way below centre, which thins the tone — and extending the beater only slows playing technique. Mind you, it didn't seem to bother Bonham.

Most players opt for a 22″ bass drum, which is the way it's been pretty well throughout rock history. As for toms, 9x13 and 16x16 became standard in America, while in Britain some odd sizes still hung around through the 1960s, such as Premier's 8x14 and deep 20x16 tom toms.

Once the trend to smaller sizes was underway it inevitably went to the extreme. The first 20″ bass drum was made by Gretsch in the 1940s for Dave Tough, the drummer with the Tommy Dorsey Orchestra, while Louie Bellson had a double Gretsch kit with two 20″ bass drums. But the 20″ (and eventually 18″) drum really found its home with the small bebop, modern and cool jazz groups of the 1950s and 1960s. In fact Gretsch, positioned close to the heart of the New York action, came on strongly from the 1940s, not only making small bass drums but also adapting hardware to make the kit compact and transportable.

MYSTICAL CYMBALISM

In collaboration with hardware supremos Walberg & Auge, Gretsch introduced 'disappearing' cymbal mounts and bass drum spurs which slid into the bass drum shell for ease of transportation. This suited the busy, small-group jazz players zooming around town, in and out of crowded basement clubs. Names like Max Roach, Art Blakey and Elvin Jones became strongly associated with Gretsch drums. Sitting well with the 20″ bass drum, the smaller 8x12 mounted drum and 14x14 floor tom — often now referred to as 'jazz' sizes — completed the familiar set-up.

An integral part of the classic Gretsch sound was the warm,

dark timbre of Turkish 'K' (Kerope) Zildjian cymbals. Gretsch had been the US importer of these cymbals from early in the century. The other type of imported cymbal came from China. Chinese cymbals are traditionally rough-and-ready with a harsher, gong-like tone. They were cheaper than the more musical, extensively hand-worked cymbals from Turkey.

The history of the modern cymbal arguably begins in 1929 when a branch of the Zildjian dynasty, led by Avedis Zildjian III, began to manufacture Turkish-style cymbals in the US, near Boston. While the imported, unpredictable, earthy Ks retained a mystical image — each cymbal being handmade and unique, prompting drummers to search for the 'perfect' one — the American branch of the family set about working directly with the indigenous drumming stars to bring cymbal making into the 20th century.

At first, you'll remember, cymbals were generally small, a 12″ example being considered large. Gradually the big band drummers of the 1930s and 1940s demanded bigger and stronger cymbals. This followed the gradual progress of the pulse from snare rolls and four-on-the-floor bass drum to the hi-hat and eventually to the top cymbal. However it was, again, the small-group bebop movement led by Kenny 'Klook' Clarke that set the pace. As the bop drummers changed to smaller drums they increasingly transferred the focus of the rhythm to the cymbals. This necessitated bigger and heavier cymbals to maintain a distinct 'ride' rhythm. Experiments went to the extremes again: 26″ rides and 18″ hi-hats, can you believe? But by the time rock came along, sizes had settled back to a more realistic 18″ or 20″ ride and 14″ hi-hats, and size-wise things have remained pretty well unaltered to the present time.

THE COMING OF ROCK

As with jazz a generation before, the early works of rock and blues were mostly the creations of black performers who went unrecognised for many years. Those performers who were successful through the sheer exuberance of their live shows had to stomach the degradation of their recorded work. Sanitised cover versions of the great Little Richard by white crooners such as Pat Boone abounded. So although many of the rock'n'roll classics by artists as diverse as Fats Domino, Little Richard, Jerry Lee Lewis and Chuck Berry are still played every day by a thousand bar bands, the drummers on these

17

Benny Goodman and Gene Krupa (above) Clarinettist Goodman and drummer Krupa personified the swing era following their success at the Palomar Ballroom, LA, in 1935. Krupa's barnstorming tom tom feature on the tune 'Sing Sing Sing' nightly brought the house down. Thereafter, star drummers became a major attraction of swing band concerts, culminating in the marathon tours de force of Buddy Rich with Artie Shaw and Tommy Dorsey. Krupa's popularity was such that by 1938 he was fronting his own band.

Slingerland Radio King (above) Krupa made Slingerland's fortune and Radio Kings were played by most big band drummers through the 1940s. The Radio King snare drum (right) is still the ultimate drum for many because of its solid maple shell. This model has brass rims and eight streamlined cigar-shaped lugs.

Benny Goodman sleeve (above) In January 1938 'The King of Swing' appeared at the prestigious New York Carnegie Hall with his Quartet (Gene Krupa, Teddy Wilson piano, and Lionel Hampton vibes) as well as his Orchestra with star guests including Count Basie.

Slingerland Radio King kit in white marine pearl c1939 *(left; see also front, below) Other than the solid maple snare, the drums are three-ply mahogany with reinforcing rings.*

The Slingerland cloud badge (below) is found on the snare and bass drums but not the toms which instead have the name engraved on the double-flanged brass rims. The small tom is mounted via a Walburg & Auge consolette with spade fitting. The Streamlined cigar lugs were fitted from around 1937 to the end of the 1930s, replacing the earlier tube lugs. Thereafter the so-called "Beavertail" single lugs were introduced, though cigar lugs were retained on the shallow snare drums. The floor tom was originally sat in a cradle basket — the legs seen here have been added later. The contemporary cymbals shown here on the Slingerland kit include a 16" Wuhan China along with various Turkish K Zildjians.

19

Slingerland Epic bass drum pedal *(right) Both bass and hi-hat pedals have Slingerland embossed on the footplates and Epic on the heel plates. The bass pedal is a handsome twin-post single-spring model with lambswool beater. The pedals are of modern design, as is much else about the kit (above), including the tripod-based cymbal stands which are by Walberg & Auge. The two hoop-mount cymbal holders (which can be positioned anywhere around the hoop) are not original, but are English "Krupa-style". The external damper on the bass drum is original, as is the double woodblock/ cowbell fitting.*

Radio King kit *(above) This modern looking kit, one of the first with a smaller bass drum, is typical of the stripped-down fashion adopted by the swing stars following Krupa. Sizes are 14x24, 9x13, 16x16, and 5½x14.*

trailblazing recordings are largely unknown. Let's put a name to a few. Little Richard's drummer on 'Tutti Frutti' (1955), 'Rip It Up' and 'Long Tall Sally' (1956) was Earl Palmer, while Chuck Berry's drummer on 'Maybellene' (1955) was Fred Below and on 'School Days' (1957) and 'Nadine' (1964) Odie Payne. The more earthy and adult blues of Chicago and Muddy Waters stayed largely black until, ironically, it was brought to the ears of white Americans by The Rolling Stones. In Chicago Muddy Waters featured drummer Elgin 'Elgie' Edmonds; Clifton James lays claim to the Bo Diddley tom tom beat; and Sam Lay was the 'double shuffle' master with Howlin' Wolf.

As well as remembering these early drummers I'd like to a take a minute to speculate on how the rhythms developed. It becomes harder by the day to imagine, but there was a time when rock *did not exist*. There was no blueprint for what the first drummers played – they made it up as they went along.

Many of these early rockers had a jazz background, imbued so much with the jazz style of playing ride cymbal with a swing – in other words a triplets-based 'ding-ding-a-ding' rhythm – that they can be heard doggedly holding a swing rhythm on fast rock'n'roll numbers where the pianist has given up and is bashing out straight eighth notes with his right hand. By 'straight' eighths I mean a brisk, even pulse as in, say, the ticking of a metronome. A classic example is 'Long Tall Sally' (1956) where Little Richard plays straight eighths on the piano while Earl Palmer plays jazz swing on the drums.

ODIE, JEROME AND DJ

On Elvis Presley's 1958 'Jailhouse Rock' drummer DJ Fontana plays a feel on his hi-hat which is some way between a swung shuffle and straight eighths. This creates a tension which would be smoothed out as rock took hold and even-eighths rhythms became unquestioned through the 1960s. (So much so that by the time we reached the 1980s the memory of this groove was in danger of being lost entirely, quantised out by the 'bpm-police' and their obsession with mechanised beats, measured in beats-per-minute. However, intuitively something felt missing, and within a few years the fashion for James Brown samples, hip hop and swing beats highlighted the obviously deep-seated need for rhythms to breathe and fluctuate. Hallelujah.)

The tension between straight eighths and triplets – 'the

beats in between' – is something which characterises the feel of Latin music, and the music of the Caribbean and southern States. And most early rock classics were recorded in the South – 'Long Tall Sally' was recorded in New Orleans, for example.

The influence of Latin rhythms has regularly been overlooked in jazz and rock. Returning once more to Krupa's promotion of the tom toms, this was partly to do with the big band rumba craze of the 1930s. And when Krupa left behind his percussion tray he nonetheless kept the Latin cowbell. Years later Chicago blues drummer Odie Payne made the cowbell his trademark feature. It was picked up by the British blues fans, crossing the Atlantic to turn up on classics like The Rolling Stones' 'Honky Tonk Women' (1969) and Free's 'All Right Now' (1970). Just as Krupa made his name with thundering tom toms, so the signature beat of early rock – the insistent tom tom figure of Bo Diddley – is the Latin clavé. Bo featured his very own maraca player, Jerome Green, in his band. Mick Jagger was never seen without his maracas in the 1960s. Oh, and the Stones' first top ten single 'Not Fade Away' (1964) had Charlie Watts pounding the Bo Diddley beat.

The fact that the rhythm of the Latin clavé could be beefed up and played on the tom toms (and any tuned instrument – check out Chuck Berry's guitar intro to 'Johnny B Goode') demonstrates that rhythm is fundamental in blues and rock music. The drums serve to enhance the rhythm and ram it home. But it's as well to remember that the drums don't actually figure in the early Delta blues of, say, Robert Johnson and they don't figure much in early rockabilly either. Although Elvis Presley has become synonymous with the rock'n'roll revolution, his first recordings were made without drums. 'That's All Right, Mama' (1954) has an unstoppable rhythm... and it's all coming from a mercilessly slapped double bass and a mean strummed guitar. Most country acts didn't use drums at all, and Elvis came to *The Louisiana Hayride* radio show with just guitar and bass. When they asked staff drummer DJ Fontana to play he says he'd heard the records and so thought he'd just keep in the background with 'a simple backbeat'. Fontana recalled: "I thought – they've got such a unique sound, so why clutter it up?"

Of course, once DJ did add the drums it was twice as exciting, and on its way to getting twice as loud. Chicago blues master Fred Below had an inkling of what was to come. He recalls tying his bass drum to his stool, something which many a rock drummer would do before the introduction of heavyweight spurs in the 1970s.

Most photos of DJ with Elvis show him playing a four-piece Gretsch kit. Herb Brochstein, now the president of Pro-Mark sticks, says this was his personal kit and that Elvis and DJ persuaded him to part with it when they walked into his Houston shop in 1954. The kit is famous for its unshaven calfskin front bass drum head, which dampened the sound. And DJ says he used goatskin heads on his toms. So early rock was performed and recorded on drums with real animal skins. I mention all this because something else we're inclined to forget is the fact that over the past 40 years the volume at which rock drummers attack their drums has increased probably by a factor of three or four. When you see early footage, the drumming looks tame by modern standards. And it is, though this doesn't mean it lacked intensity – but that's for another book. The important point I'm getting to here is that, although it was settled in layout, the drum kit wasn't prepared for the barrage of violence that awaited it just around the corner. And things could not have happened the way they did but for the perfectly timed arrival of the plastic drum head.

THE PLASTIC HEAD

William Ludwig likes to tell the story of how, right up to the start of the 1960s, Ludwig and Slingerland, based in Chicago adjacent to vast livestock markets, would compete to get the best skins. Drum making was to an extent determined by the availability of good skins.

Attempts at producing synthetic skins or 'heads' had been made way back in the 19th century. But nothing serious happened until the early 1950s when experiments were made with a polyester film called Mylar, developed by Du Pont during World War II as a heat-resistant film for night-time reconnaissance flights. The first Mylar drum head was apparently made as early as 1953 by Jim Irwin for jazz drummer Sonny Greer.

Through the middle 1950s there developed a race to make the idea of a synthetic head commercially viable. An early runner was Marion 'Chick' Evans – the present Evans Heads company bears his name. Both Ludwig and Premier were hot on his heels. However, it was Remo Belli in collaboration with

a chemist named Sam Muchnick who developed the Remo Weather King drum head. It was introduced at the Chicago NAMM musical instruments trade show in June 1957, and went into production that autumn. Remo was destined to become the world's leading manufacturer of synthetic drum heads.

Although the concept of using Mylar was evidently a winner, there were technical problems, firstly concerning how to 'clinch' the head into the hoop so that it wouldn't pull out, and, thereafter, of finding the exact formulation of Mylar appropriate for stick bashing. By the turn of the 1960s these problems had been overcome sufficiently well so that over the next few years drummers of all persuasions were gradually converted. Not only were plastic heads stronger than animal skin, they were weatherproof, consistent, cheaper and could be produced in vast quantities.

OVER IN BRITAIN

In the mid 1940s the British popular and jazz music scene was way behind that of America, and console kits were still commonly to be seen in action. Furthermore, import restrictions introduced soon after World War II made it virtually impossible to get American gear in the UK, and even homemade instruments were rare.

Veteran drummer Roy Holliday, who later became Pearl's manager in Britain, had to get a Board of Trade 'certificate for non essential goods' in order to buy a kit and get work. He bought a British Ajax kit because "it looked American". A few American drums were smuggled into Britain from New York by drummers working the cruise liners, or by the handful of jazz musicians who made the pilgrimage to America to see how they measured up with the greats. Roy Holliday: "In the late 1940s to mid 1950s guys took their Premier kits over in cases and swapped them for American kits to bring back." The drummers would also have to swap the badges to fool the customs officers.

Through the 1950s the big swing bands gradually lost ground in Britain, although Palais (dancehall) bands played a variety of dance styles from quicksteps to cha-chas, as evidenced by the stiffly humourless drum method books of the time. But while America forged ahead with modern and cool jazz, for some reason in Britain a revival of interest in early New Orleans-style jazz led to a popular movement – the trad

Brian Bennett (above and left) Bennett is seen on stage (above) with Gene Vincent at the Albert Hall in 1960; as a member of Marty Wilde's Wild Cats, Bennett also backed Gene Vincent and Eddie Cochran, and is playing his black Trixon kit which he went on to use when he first joined The Shadows in 1961. Bennett is also seen, pre-roadies, on Bexhill railway station (left) during the same 1960 package tour, photographed by guitar session legend Big Jim Sullivan. And you thought they were joking when they said they carried their own gear?

Trixon Luxus 0/200 kit in red pearl c1965 (above) Rims are turned over-and-in like later Slingerlands (earlier Trixons had die-cast rims), and the rectangular lugs are set on black plastic plinths. The bass drum has original disappearing spurs, tom mount and bracket for a disappearing cymbal stand – all with 'ship-form' baseplates. The 5x14 Trixon snare (left) has the internal parallel action that was often seen in 1960s European snare drums.

Bill Haley and Trixon Speedfire 0/700-3 kit (above) Trixon catalogues were as colourful as their drums were show-stopping (modern manufacturers, please take note). Here, in a 1960s catalogue shot, Bill Haley and the drummer from the Comets show off in regal style the elliptical 0/701 bass drum which, once again for Trixon, embodies two different sounds in one instrument. The egg-shaped bass drum had a central partition, and two separate pedals could be mounted along the flat bottom rim. The 0/700 series kits had a rail console with up to five 'wrong way'-mounted concert toms and a huge Lionel Hampton 18x20 floor tom.

Trixon Telstar in Blue Croco c1965 (right) The Model 2000 Telstar (or Vox Fanjet in the US) had 'twin sound', implying the drums could be played either way up, though this was only feasible with the small tom. The bass drum and floor tom have the same size shells, 16" widening to 20". Note the earlier style of 'arrowhead' die-cast lugs.

Karl-Heinz Weimer with Buddy Rich (above) Weimer (left) was 'Mr Trixon'; he persuaded Buddy Rich to endorse Trixon drums in early 1967.

(short for traditional) jazz boom. While the fledgling rock'n'rollers had no chance unless they could muster a halfway decent Elvis impersonation, these poor devils had Louis Armstrong for their vocal inspiration, and waistcoated, bowler-hatted jazz musicians competed to produce the most excruciating version of the great man's hammed-up vocals.

SKIFFLE TO BEAT

The first signs of the British do-it-yourself mentality in pop music came when some breakaway trad musicians, led by Lonnie Donegan with his hit 'Rock Island Line' (1956), had unexpected success with a rough-and-ready variant of early rock/rockabilly called skiffle. This was swiftly replaced by the coming of the 'beat' groups, presaged by The Shadows, the backing group of Britain's foremost Elvis wannabee, Cliff Richard. The Shads scored massive success with the guitar, rhythm guitar, bass and drums line-up which was to become the mainstay of the beat group era, as adopted by The Beatles but minus the cut-price Elvis out front.

The Shadows' success away from Cliff was based largely on the still new thrill of the electric guitar, which had replaced the saxophone as the lead instrument of rock. For a while the small-group guitar-led sound was sufficiently novel to do away with the need for the vocalist, and promoted a fashion for instrumental hits in the early 1960s. The American guitarist Duane Eddy was king of the twang, influencing The Ventures in the States and The Shadows in Britain.

The Ventures' drummer played a Gretsch kit with sparkle finish, an instrument of unimaginable sexiness to the glamour-starved musicians of late-1950s Britain, where skiffle groups generally went to work with a rhythm section consisting of a washboard and a tea-chest bass. Sure enough, The Shadows' drummer Tony Meehan became the first high profile owner of a Gretsch champagne sparkle kit in Britain. It was a taster for what would come over the next decade.

The Shadows' bespectacled, gangling guitarist Hank Marvin modelled himself on the bespectacled, gangling Buddy Holly, and with his distinctively melodic tremolo-swamped Fender sound and any number of instrumental hits Marvin became Britain's first proper guitar hero, several years before Eric Clapton. The Shadows were a class act, not least because of their drummers Tony Meehan and, from late 1961, Brian

Bennett, both fine players with jazz skills who nonetheless were youthful enough to appeal to the new teenage audience. Bennett's British role models were the big band and show drummers like Kenny Clare and Eric Delaney. When I asked Bennett why he went into rock, the simple answer was that the big bands were all but dead — there weren't any jobs. And luckily he was at the right age to identify with rock. Although The Shads never made it big in the States, Meehan and Bennett were *the* first role models for the generation of British drummers like Phil Collins and Cozy Powell who followed on and achieved undreamed-of international success.

Then, as now, Premier was the top drum company in Britain. Ajax was some way behind, although it was used by several top pros (including Andy White, the session drummer remembered forever for playing on the album version of the Beatles' first record 'Love Me Do' in 1962). Ajax were made by Boosey & Hawkes and were distinguished by their bullet-shaped lugs and die-cast rims. They had an impressive line of snare drums with great names including the Snapper, the Pipper and Pipperette, and the exceptionally thin Cooperette. Shallow snare drums were very popular; Ringo Starr, for example, had a John Grey Autocrat 3x14 drum just prior to joining The Beatles.

Ajax cymbals were also common at this time although they were nothing to boast about. Premier had earlier imported Zildjians to the UK, but following the war these were rare, so most drummers had to put up with homemade or Italian cymbals stamped with vaguely Eastern sounding names like Rassem and Symara. Premier made Krut cymbals — 'Turk' backwards — although some thought it referred to the sound the cymbals made. Premier also made Zyn, Super Zyn and Five Star Super Zyn (the latter not half bad and made from genuine 'B20' cymbal alloy) and supplied lines to other manufacturers.

With money scarce, but live music in clubs, pubs, theatres and concert halls much more widespread, there were many more amateur drummers. Today the needs of new drummers are catered for by numerous Taiwan-made budget kits, but in those days most things were manufactured in Britain, so there was a market for cheap and cheerful kits from old familiar names. Top line kits from Carlton, Ajax and Premier were complemented by their respective entry-level lines: Gigster, Edgware and Olympic. The cheaper kits often had the same

Ringo kit c1961 *(below) According to Sotheby's auction house, Ringo played this kit with Rory Storm & The Hurricanes prior to joining The Beatles.*

Ringo Starr's Premier kit c1961 *(left) This kit, sold by Sotheby's in London in 1995, is similar to Ringo's first Beatles kit with the obvious exception of the snare drum, a white pearl John Grey Autocrat 3x14. Many players of the period favoured these shallower snare drums. As rock got louder the inadequacy of the typical snare drum stand became apparent. The feeble fold-out flat-strip metal arms* would gradually bend under the increasing power of the back beat until the vertical centre post smashed through the bottom head. Also, check the infamous Premier 245 folding (when you least expected it) tripod stool. This item made early-1960s drumming about as secure as riding a penny farthing bicycle. Sizes are 14x20, 8x12, 16x16. The cymbals are 15" Ajax hi-hats and 16" Ajax crash — not original, but typical.

Premier '58

With the 14"x14" floor-tom, this outfit has set the smaller drum fashion. Easy to handle and quick to set up. Ideal for busy 'in-town' drummers. Shown here in Premier's exclusive Mahogany but the outfit may, of course, be had in any Premier finish.

	No.
Bass Drum, 20"x17" (14" shell) with disappearing spurs	130
Snare Drum, 14"x4"	10
Tom-tom, 14"x14", with 3 legs	435
Tom-tom, 12"x8"	442
Bass Drum Pedal	259
Hi-hat	289
Snare Drum Stand	300
Cymbal Stand with Tilter	304
Tom-tom Holder, disappearing	389
Bass Drum Post	469
Cowbell and Clamp	771

CYMBALS 1 pr. 14" Super-Zyn Hi-hats / 18" Super-Zyn

OUTFIT
'58' with 20" Bass Drum
'B58' with 22" Bass Drum
'C58' with 18" Bass Drum

EXCLUSIVE PREMIER FINISHES *(far more beautiful than it's possible to reproduce on paper).* Extra thickness gives you the deep, lustrous finish so exclusively Premier. And longer life too. All plating in Premier 'Diamond' Chromium. All B.D. hoops except B finished in high gloss black.

GLITTERS R Red   C Silver   A Aquamarine   DUROPLASTICS W White   B

Premier 58 kit 1966 *(above)* This kit in Premier's catalogue is in the same 'mahogany' Duroplastic finish as Ringo's first Beatles kit. Ringo played the 4" Royal Ace snare drum as featured here, but his kit was more likely a 54 model with the larger 16" floor tom. In the 1960s, Premier kits were of excellent quality, and while often seen as slightly old-fashioned (the flush-based stands and rubberised

footpedals had a "dance band" image), the die-cast components with their diamond chrome plating were world class. The "disappearing" tom holder allowed some vertical adjustment (see kit, right) while the disappearing spurs did little to prevent forward creeping movement. Kits came equipped with Premier's own factory-produced Super Zyn cymbals and Everplay Extra heads.

John Grey Broadway kit in turquoise glitter 1965 *(above)* A typical semi-pro British kit of the beat era, the Broadway Super 9051 retailed in 1965 at £79/14s/7d (£79.73; about $127) and comprised a 15x20 bass drum plus single-headed 8x12 and 16x16 tom toms. This was John Grey's budget version of the Autocrat: note the six (not eight) tension lugs on snare and bass drum. The Autospeed footpedal had a leather strap and pressed steel footplate. In keeping with many British kits then, rims were die-moulded. Heads were John Grey "Headmasters", cymbals "Kamalas".

Olympic 1182 snare drum shell c1965 *(left)* Olympic has been the budget "little brother" to Premier from its inception in 1937 until the present day. This 5½x14 shell was of the same quality as evident in the full-price Premier — it had a thin birch shell, with beechwood reinforcing rings. Premier claimed they used a "400 year old English method" of shell manufacture. Savings were made in the Olympic's cheaper lugs (it had six rather than eight), strainer, and rims.

John Grey Autocrat snare drum *(right)* The 3x14 model 524 wood-shell drum had die-cast rims and slot-head tension bolts, which was all typical of most British manufacturers until the American square-headed bolts and triple-flanged rims took over.

AUTOCRAT NARROW SHELL SNARE
Model 524 14" x 3" (36 x 7·5 cms.)
A lightweight snare drum preferred by many for its superb brush response and par... small band and recording work.

AJAX STACCATO OUTFIT

A compact kit featuring the latest in drum sizes. Ideal for the gig drummer playing one-nighters. Kit comprises:

4904	20 x 14" Bass Drum.	
4983	14 x 5" Snare Drum.	
4981	12" x 8" Tom-Tom.	
4985	14 x 14" Tom-Tom with legs.	
4942	T/T Holder.	
7602	Snare Drum Stand.	
4943	B/D Cymbal mount.	
7600	Hi-Hat Pedal.	
7362	Bass Drum Pedal.	
4940	1 pair Spurs.	
7232	1 pair Sticks.	
7799	1 pair Brushes.	
6990	Bass Drum Anchor.	
6901	Ajax Staccato outfit without cymbals	£146. 0. 0
6901C	Ajax Staccato outfit with two 14" and one 16" Ajax cymbals	£154. 18. 6

Ajax Nu Sound kit late 1960s
(below) This kit is in Burgundy Ripple finish and, with sizes 12x22, 9x13, 16x16 and 5x14 wood-shell snare, is a hybrid of the five-drum Forte (which had an extra 12" tom and Metasonic 5x14 metal-shell snare) and the four-drum Staccato (which had the 14x20 bass drum and 14x14 floor tom). Interestingly, the 22" bass drum was 12" deep while the 20" was 14" deep. The shells have reinforcing hoops and inside are stained a slightly reddish colour, described by Ajax as 'Satin Mahogany'. The new Ajax 'A' design appears on the two bass drum cymbal mounts and the disappearing tom mount. The Nu Sound also came with flush-based stands and the Accelerator floating-action type bass drum pedal.

Andy White (above) Ajax endorser White was booked by George Martin to cover for new-boy Ringo on the album version of The Beatles' UK debut single 'Love Me Do' in September 1962.

Ajax Nu Sound catalogue
(below) The radical Nu Sound line ran from 1967 to 1970 and ideally should have taken over from the English Rogers. With triple-flanged rims and the 'A' motif stamped into the new lugs the drums had a more American look than Premier but they proved to be Ajax's swan song. Finishes included black, red and blue pearls.

Rogers (English) kit c1967
(right; see also front, far right bottom) Rogers kits from the 1960s and 1970s often had astronomical names like Constellation and Starlighter. This kit has the Constellation (or later Headliner) set-up of 20, 12 and 16, though it has a Dyna-Sonic snare drum rather than the cheaper Power-Tone suggested in the catalogues. It also has two cymbal mounts on the bass drum. Rogers made two types of cymbal mount: the Swiv-O-Matic 'disappearing' design (here stamped 'Made In England') and the hinged Knobby-fitting design. The improved Beavertail lugs were introduced around the mid 1960s; the earlier rectangular bread-and-butter lugs had a tendency to crack. The thin shells have reinforcing hoops and are nicely finished inside with a clear lacquer. American Rogers shells generally have a grey paint/fleck interior finish.

DYNA-SONIC
SERIAL NO. 42511
CUSTOM BUILT

Rogers U.S.A.
DRUMS WITH SWIV-O-MATIC
MADE IN UK UNDER LICENCE

Rogers DRUM PEDALS

the fantastic new
Rogers Swiv-O-Matic Pedal

Revolutionary new design! Cuts foot fatigue! Adjusts to your natural position! Gives smoothest action ever!

Notice how this pedal adjusts to you—to your foot—to your drums—to your style.

★ You raise or lower beater action without changing length of stroke—so you get the exact sound you want from any drum.

★ You adjust length of stroke without changing beater height.

Rogers (English) catalogue
(above) By the early 1960s American Rogers with Swiv-O-Matic hardware were the most advanced (and expensive) drums. In the UK, Rogers were made under license by Boosey & Hawkes (noted in the small print here).

Rogers Swiv-O-Matic footpedal
(right) This unit could be mounted at an angle to the bass drum and the hoop clamp left permanently on the drum. The upturned spring allowed easy reach from the sitting position – and this was a feature that would be copied by Pearl in the 1970s. The pedal was available in two forms: one with hinged heel (as shown here), or with adjustable single-piece footboard (see kit, above).

Pete York (below) As demonstrated by this ad from the British musicians' newspaper Melody Maker in 1966, York provided the musicianly face of English Rogers through his prominence as the skilful, jazzy drummer with The Spencer Davis Group. The band also featured a teenage Steve Winwood on keyboards and guitar, as well as his brother Muff Winwood on bass. Later, Pete York moved from Britain to Germany, where he fronted his own drumming series on television.

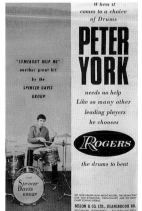

Dave Clark 1964 (above) The Dave Clark Five's enormous success both in Britain and the US helped secure Rogers' cut of the expanding rock market. Clark's eye-catching red glitter five-piece kit featured a 20" bass drum, and 12" and 13" toms mounted the 'wrong' way around. The Londoner V kit later featured Beavertail lugs and the dual Swiv-O-Matic tom mount.

Dyna-Sonic snare drum (below) Introduced around 1960, this model was reputedly designed for Buddy Rich. The special rib-strengthened shell was of chrome-plated brass.

Rogers (English) kit c1967
(front, left) This pristine English Rogers kit is played regularly by drummer Cleve Key (hence the 'CK' logo on the bass head) in Birmingham, England. All the stands and drums are as originally supplied with the kit. The cymbals are: Avedis Zildjian 20" Ping Ride; 16" crash, 18" crash and 14" hi-hats; 8" 'K' Zildjian splash. There was a strong connection between English Rogers and Ajax, demonstrated by the 1967 English Rogers and the Ajax Nu Sound catalogues listing the same finishes. Also, English Rogers kits could be bought with cheaper Ajax pedals.

shells but fewer, more basic lugs and sometimes single-headed toms. There were a number of other drum brand-names that were popular in Britain through the 1960s, including Autocrat, Beverley, Rose-Morris, Shaftesbury and Broadway.

TRIXON LAUNCHES TELSTAR

As with everything else in the 1960s a major change was on the way. It had started with the arrival of exciting new Trixon drums from Hamburg in West Germany, the brainchild of an ingenious drum manufacturer named Karl-Heinz Weimer. They were brought over to Britain by Ivor Arbiter, who was to become a key figure in the story of British rock drums. Arbiter started out with his father Joe, a professional saxophone player, when they opened the Paramount Musical Instrument Company in Shaftesbury Avenue at the heart of central London's theatre district in 1956. With the rock scene just about to go ballistic, guitars were in short supply and an extra source was found in Holland.

Arbiter explains: "About 1957 I met a man in Holland called Koek Koek. He introduced me to Trixon drums and suggested I try to sell them in England. I went to the factory in Hamburg and brought a few kits back. We got Phil Seamen [reckoned to be Britain's greatest jazz drummer] and for the first time Premier and Ajax had a bit of a competitor."

British drummers, starved of something new, quickly latched on to Trixon. Brian Bennett of The Shadows explains: "Ivor and his dad were a great help to young musicians and they helped me buy the black Trixon which I had for about four years. It was of good wood, and was loud, sturdy... and bloody heavy! I had the Trixon for the first year of The Shadows." Before joining The Shadows, Bennett had been a member of Marty Wilde's Wild Cats and also backed visiting American rock legends Eddie Cochran and Gene Vincent.

For a while all the early British rockers transferred to Trixon – Clem Cattini with Billy Fury and Johnny Kidd & The Pirates, Bob Henrit with Adam Faith's Roulettes (today he's with The Kinks), and even The Hollies' Bobby Elliott, who played a red Trixon. Henrit says, "Trixon overtook Premier for a while. They had a very cool image, while poor old Ajax and the rest had a dance band image."

Weimer certainly had drive and ambition. Amazingly he eventually persuaded The Guv'nor, Buddy Rich, to endorse

Trixon in 1967, albeit very briefly. Buddy played a Luxus outfit with a metal shell snare drum. Inevitably Trixon made an impression in the States, where Buddy's kit was badged as Vox. Vox kits were seen on stage with James Brown, and Bill Haley's drummer featured memorably in Trixon catalogues.

Trixon, anticipating the wacky 1960s, will always be venerated for two of the craziest kits ever successfully marketed. The Speedfire had a row of up to five backward-mounted concert toms racked over an elliptical egg-shaped bass drum, giving the impression of a small and large bass drum joined like Siamese twins. Inside was a divider, and two separate bass pedals were mounted on the flat bottom rim.

The other unusual Trixon kit was the conical-shelled Telstar, known as the Vox Fan Jet in the States. The real Telstar was a communications satellite launched by America in 1962, the first to relay live TV transmissions between the US and Europe. And 'Telstar' was also the name of the hi-tech-for-the-day instrumental created by Joe Meek, touted as Britain's answer to the American 'wall of sound' producer Phil Spector. As house drummer for Meek, Clem Cattini was drummer with The Tornados who recorded 'Telstar' (1962) which became a number one hit in Britain. 'Telstar' then went on to become the first British number one hit on the American charts. Cattini, however, was far too wily to play a Telstar kit, which he knew would never sound as good as it looked. Cattini stuck with his conventional white pearl Luxus outfit. It may be, in fact, that it was Weimer's outrageous vision which eventually became his downfall. As Brian Bennett sums it up: "Trixon lost the plot when they did the conical kit."

PEGGY SUE AND THE PARADIDDLES

Another young man whom Trixon impressed was Gerry Evans, who left school in 1961 to work at Arbiter's Paramount store. Evans enthuses: "Karl-Heinz Weimer was such an innovator. Trixon wasn't fantastic but it was progressive. For example, all the stands had spring-loaded legs, an idea that was later copied by Ajax." But the pragmatic Ivor Arbiter sums it up: "Weimer was ahead of his time and he developed a lot of die-cast stuff in nice shapes and forms. We did quite well with Trixon, but drumming was getting heavier and Trixon started to make some silly mistakes." Perhaps Weimer went too far too fast. Nonetheless, the damage to the British drum industry was done. The pioneering rockers with their Trixon kits had got a taste of something exciting and new beyond the too familiar Ajax and Premier, who through no real fault of their own were identified with the pre-beat era. The new breed of drummers needed a break from tradition to go with the new approaches to drumming they were hearing on imported records. Things started to move even faster when they made contact with their American heroes.

Bob Henrit, playing the Albert Hall with Adam Faith in support of Buddy Holly, realised that there was some catching up to be done. "When I first saw Jerry [Allison, Buddy's drummer] I thought it was ridiculous! He was a schooled drummer and we weren't. Every drummer played 'Peggy Sue' hand to hand, but he played it as a paradiddle – we didn't even know what a paradiddle was. And the way he played on 'Oh Boy' was subtle. He was putting something into rock which we weren't seeing. We were emulating him without realising what the hell he was doing."

Information was quickly shared. Henrit again: "Brian Bennett backed Eddie Cochran when he played in Britain. Eddie was moving into straight eighths, although 'Twenty Flight Rock' was definitely a shuffle or jazz feel. 'Summertime Blues' had this feel which to us was magic, and Eddie showed it to Brian. Brian learned it and it filtered down to us. It had upbeats on the bass drum and that was quite alien to us then. Then the straight eighths came in and Brian and Tony Meehan and I started to play 'two-handers'," says Henrit. A 'two-hander' was a sort of straightened-out version of the double-handed unison shuffle.

These bass drum upbeats were new to generations who had only known the feeble four-on-the-floor of dance bands. Gerry Evans remembers two drummers on the London scene who first made him aware of the rock'n'roll possibilities of the bass drum. "The first time I heard the bass drum was in 1962," he recalls, "and it was Carlo Little with Screaming Lord Sutch & The Savages, who were amazing at the time. I also heard it from Frank Farley with Johnny Kidd & The Pirates. It was like a cannon going off! Up until then it was hardly anything." Bob Henrit also remembers Bobby Woodman, dubbed 'The Wild Man of Rock', who played with Vince Taylor and Screaming Lord Sutch, and used a double bass drum kit that had lights inside. "His cymbals were really awful, they had great gouges

out of them," Henrit remembers of Woodman the wild man, "but in effect he was Keith Moon ten years before his time."

How Do You Do It?

Outside the happening London scene, gear was more basic. Drummers in the provinces made do with what they could get. The Silver Beetles called on the services of top Liverpool sticks man Johnny 'Hutch' Hutchinson to fill in for the absent Tommy Moore at an audition for Britain's top pop mogul Larry Parnes. In a telling photo an aloof looking Hutch is seen sitting on a wooden bar stool playing a terrible single-headed drum kit. But it did not take long before The Beatles found their own full-time drummer, the affluent Pete Best, who bought a respectable white pearl Premier.

Ringo Starr, already a name on the Liverpool scene but still playing Butlin's holiday camps with Rory Storm & The Hurricanes, had a mahogany (plastic) finish Premier with Krut and Ajax cymbals and the previously mentioned 3″ Autocrat snare drum. The famous Dezo Hoffmann pictures of the early Abbey Road recording sessions of September 4th 1962 show Ringo with his new band playing a similar mahogany Premier, again with a shallow snare drum – this time a Premier Royal Ace 4″ wood shell.

Ludwig and Ringo

The early 1960s found Ivor Arbiter in the tricky situation of providing Premier's main competition, but becoming increasingly disillusioned with Trixon. "We were easing off on Trixon because of the quality problems," Arbiter explains. He says that while the hardware looked OK it wasn't too strong – the nut boxes would come off, for example. But Arbiter had been impressed by Ludwig drums and couldn't understand why they weren't available in Britain. "I went to a trade show in New York and realised, with import duty and purchase tax, that they were going to have to sell at twice the price of British drums. Bill Ludwig reckoned there was no way we'd sell them. But we got a few over and then we opened Drum City."

Almost exactly a decade after Remo Belli had opened his Drum City in Hollywood, Ivor Arbiter opened his Drum City at 114 Shaftesbury Avenue in central London in 1962. Drum City salesman Gerry Evans remembers: "It was fabulous. The day it opened we had Slingerland, Gretsch, Ludwig, Trixon, the

...for sheer beauty and Rich tone
LUDWIG...most famous name on drums!

This outfit especially designed for Buddy Rich by Ludwig Drum Co., chicago, illinois

Buddy Rich (left) Rich influenced every drummer who heard him or, even better, saw him play. A child prodigy, Rich started off as "Traps The Drum Wonder", playing Ludwig & Ludwig. From 1940 to his death in 1987 he was recognised as the great genius of swing band drumming. He played WFL/Ludwig drums from 1946 to 1959 and again from 1977 to 1980, before finishing his career on a kit of restored Slingerland Radio Kings.

Brian Bennett's Ludwig Super Classic kit c1963 (front, above) British importer Ivor Arbiter wisely presented both Brian Bennett and Ringo Starr with Ludwig kits in 1963.

32

WONDERFUL LAND MIDNIGHT
STARS FELL ON STOCKTON 36-34-36
mono
WONDERFUL
LAND
OF
THE
SHADOWS

Shadows sleeve (above) The Shadows with drummer Brian Bennett (and before him Tony Meehan) were the top domestic role models for the emerging British beat group generation of the early 1960s. Bennett and Meehan had considerable skill and, since the Shads were an instrumental group, both drummers had the chance to shine. Here Bennett models the white pearl Premier 4" Royal Ace snare drum.

Brian Bennett's Ludwig Super Classic kit c1963

(below; see also front, left) The shallow 12x22 bass drum of Bennett's sparkle silver kit allowed the front head to be retained without "boom" (check the intro to 1964's 'Flingel Bunt'). Cymbals include a 'K' Zildjian ride and a large China with rivets.

Ringo Starr

(right) Much of The Beatles' early excitement derived from Ringo's unerring beat, great taste and unique time feel. Later he turned his shortcomings in technique and his left-handed tendency to further musical effect, using fewer beats in his fills to make them melodic rather than merely drumistic. He's seen here with a Ludwig Downbeat oyster black pearl kit (20", 12", 14" and 5" Classic wood snare).

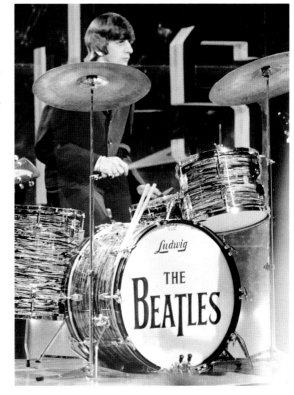

Ludwig brass shell Supraphonic 400 c1961

(below) Brian Bennett's 400 is one of the rare early models with a chromed brass shell (heavier than the standard aluminium) and no serial number. The drum is modified with a Rogers PowerTone strainer. Of the Supraphonic's notorious tendency to work loose its tension bolts, Bennett comments: "A trick I learned was to wrap cotton around every other bolt thread, and it wouldn't move an inch."

Consolette mount

(above) The original consolette mount was manufactured by Walberg & Auge from the late 1930s right through to the 1970s. Earlier designs (eg WFL's Clipper) had a spade slip-on fitting. Here the 'L' bracket slots into a receiver block on the small tom.

English drums and Paiste, the only place in the country with that selection. Nothing would have happened without Ivor – and not because he had lots of money. He was an absolute pioneer, very much a self-made man."

So Arbiter was geared up for the expanding market... but not even he could have guessed what was to happen now. From separate conversations with Arbiter and Evans a story emerges. This is how Arbiter remembers it: "One day [Beatles' manager] Brian Epstein walked into Drum City and said he'd got a band that's going to be big. So he came round the office with Ringo and I tried to get shot of some Trixon drums. But on my desk there was a swatch of Ludwig colours and Ringo said, 'That's what I want.'"

Gerry Evans was in the shop. "I think Ringo originally wanted plain black, but it would take six weeks on special order," he recalls. "So he was told to go round to the drum shop, where he sees the black oyster Ludwig and says, 'That's it!' The other thing which was very important was this kit was a Downbeat, the smaller sizes. He's only a little guy – and he sat behind it and looked big. It had a 5x14 wood snare, 20" bass drum and 14" floor tom."

Arbiter continues: "And so we did Ringo a deal, and then Brian said, 'Can you get the bass drum head painted for us for TV?'" With his legendary business flair, Arbiter sensed an opportunity. "There was this guy called Eddie Stokes who painted all the bass drum heads, and I got him up to my office and said we've got to design this Beatles thing. Apparently they're going to be big, so why don't we make Ludwig big as well? And I'm sure I designed the big 'B' and Eddie did the rest. That head recently sold for just over £27,000 [about $43,500]!"

According to Beatles' photographer Dezo Hoffmann, Ringo first appeared in public with his Ludwig kit in June 1963 at the Playhouse Theatre for a recording of the radio programme *Easy Beat* (with just one overhead mike, by the way). Gerry Evans delivered the Ludwig and took Ringo's old mahogany Premier in part exchange.

"The part exchange was £120 [$190]," Evans remembers, "and the Ludwig was worth about £238 [$380], so Ivor swallowed the £100 [$160] difference for publicity, which wasn't a bad deal. The Premier wasn't actually that old – he'd bought it in Liverpool – so I took it back and immediately we ripped off the front head which he'd written 'Beatles' on by

hand, and we threw that in the bin! An Australian chap came in looking for a secondhand Premier kit, and we said we've got this kit off a band called The Beatles. He'd actually heard of them, and he took it for £120 [$190]. As far as I know he took it back to Australia." Evans adds: "I got involved in another two Beatles Ludwigs before I left Drum City. The second kit was donated by Ludwig. Then the third kit was a Super Classic with the bigger sizes – 22", 13" and 16" – because they needed more volume."

Arbiter remembers that the Ringo kit was a tremendous boost for Ludwig. On TV, Eddie Stokes' logo made it look like 'Ludwig Beatles', and Premier and Ajax suddenly took a back seat in the British drum market. Everyone wanted a Ludwig like Ringo's. Gerry Evans recalls selling 14 kits a day at Drum City – and six of those would be Ludwig.

MICK'S MARACAS

Perhaps because of the sheer number of Ludwig kits being produced, Ludwig ran into quality problems. Bill Ludwig has said that Ludwig were making 600 kits a week for three years during the Beatles boom. Arbiter remembers disgruntled customers coming back to the shop: "They used to say: 'Why are the shells *oval*?' I'd say it's because they're all handmade... and who said the shell has to be round anyway? It's the sound that matters! The way we sold the Ludwigs was: 'Twice the price but twice the sound'."

Evans was in the front line. "The oval Ludwig bass drums became famous, but it was no joke for us at the store. We had this wonderful situation with Ludwig, and then suddenly these bass drums started coming back. Someone would buy an expensive kit and then they couldn't fit the bass drum head. I don't know what went wrong. Maybe it was the shipping? But it remedied itself after a few months."

Ringo was the first of a large number of famous customers Evans assisted. Number two was the Rolling Stones' Charlie Watts. "I sold Charlie a secondhand Ludwig kit on HP ('hire purchase' credit) because he didn't have any money. It was a blue oyster Super Classic, and he loved it. So far as I know he's still got it. Charlie used to bring this Mick Jagger to the shop with him, and all he was interested in was our maracas. So I'd wrap them up in brown paper and sellotape, his for 28/3d [about £1.42, or $2.30]."

MOON THE LOON

While all this was going on, Gerry Evans, himself a drummer, was trying to help out a young pal. "My best friend at the time was Keith Moon. We were the same age, and he lived in Wembley [north London] and started to work up town with his dad as a plasterer's mate. He was about 15, and even then he used to cause havoc. He never had a kit but I got in a little pop group and Keith would set my drums up. The agreement was that for that, I'd let him play. But the trouble was as soon as he got on the drums it was all hell let loose – he always played like that, from day one. The rest of the band used to hate it.

"So Keith wasn't very popular, but I got on well with him. Eventually I told him that we had a secondhand Premier which he could have for £75 [$120]. His dad signed the forms and he bought it on HP out of his plasterer's mate wages. It was an old fashioned blue pearl kit, and that was his first drum kit. When I was away on holiday he took my place in the band, The Escorts, and they lost all our gigs."

Moon regularly dropped by Drum City to meet Evans after work. "We used to go home on the Bakerloo line (underground railway) from Piccadilly Circus to Wembley Park and we'd change at Baker Street where there was a steep escalator. He always used to go into this shop in the station, and on this occasion he bought a pound of coffee beans, went to the top of the escalator and poured the beans down the central reservation. This was in the rush hour. The beans gathered momentum and as all the people were queuing to get on at the bottom suddenly they were pelted with what seemed like bullets. It was quite creative. He'd shot a thousand people at once with all these beans, and people were actually falling on the floor. But this was normal, something like this happened every night. And when Keith got on the drum kit he played like a maniac. The ironical thing was that it turned out so good."

Bob Henrit: "Moon would sit in at The Cromwellian [London night-club and star's hangout] and he would play everything like [The Who's] 'My Generation' – whether it was 'My Girl' or 'Walking the Dog'. Keith didn't give a shit which hand he finished on, so long as he could hit something on the down beat."

Although Moon stayed touchingly loyal to Premier throughout his career, Ringo's conversion to Ludwig had started a revolution. The accepted wisdom of the day was that American drums were louder. Evans says that the change to the American kits was mainly because of fashion – but it was also the sound and the volume, and there was no doubt that the American kits sounded better and brighter. Ironically, as The Beatles conquered the pop world, British drum companies were for the most part swept aside, stranded by an unequal struggle that most would lose by the end of the 1960s.

Premier survived, with wounded pride and the loss of their number one position, largely because the overall market was expanding fast. But Premier had also been genuinely innovative, and there was no doubt that they turned out well made products. They'd had a major boost during World War II when they were engaged in specialist work on radar and gunsights. Their west London factory was burnt out in a 1940 bomb raid, but the company was important enough to be transplanted to the central England city of Leicester.

The high standards of engineering which Premier were forced to adopt during the war were put to immediate use when peace returned. From the mid 1940s Premier became renowned for the quality of their die-cast components. The first Premier cymbal stands were solid efforts, and for a while they led the way with fold-out flush-based stands, which even had die-cast legs. Unfortunately Premier were so proud of this concept they insisted on sticking with flush-based stands right through to the 1970s, long after most other companies had moved on to more convenient and easy-to-set-up tripod bases.

However, during the late 1950s and early 1960s Premier drums attained a surprising degree of popularity with American jazz drummers. Eminent players including Philly Jo Jones, Sam Woodyard (playing double bass drums with Duke Ellington) and Kenny Clarke all enthusiastically played Premier. One factor in this was the quality of Premier's die-cast rims, a feature they had in common with Gretsch, although Gretsch's rims are rather deeper. Premier's rims also featured 'diamond chrome' plating which was unquestionably superior to Ludwig's. In fact the chrome on the Ludwig Supraphonic snare drums was forever bubbling and capable of inflicting nasty little splinter-type wounds. This was partly because they had aluminium alloy shells.

With Ludwig stealing the limelight, Premier tried to hang on to the big names by offering high profile advertising. One extremely persuasive selling point was the fact that the

Camco ad 1965 (below) Dennis Wilson of The Beach Boys was Camco's best known endorser. For those reading in mono, this kit is in Blue Moiré.

Ludwig Super Classic kit in Oyster Blue Pearl c1966 (below right; see also front, right) This kit rested unused in Clem Cattini's garage for many years, plastered with stickers including 'The Rhythm Section' (shades of Hal Blaines' Cutting Crew), from when Cattini worked with renowned 1960s sessioneers like bassists John Paul Jones and Herbie 'Walk On The Wild Side' Flowers, and guitarist Jimmy Page. Other stickers atop the bass drum include a 'panic button' and 'Dolby Stereo switch'. The original consolette is replaced by a Ludwig double mount. Note the Rogers Swiv-O-Matic bass pedal. Sizes are 14x22, 9x13, 16x16, and 5x14 Supraphonic 400 snare drum (dated January 13th 1966). The bottom heads were removed from the drums during the 1970s.

Ludwig kit (front, above) British session legend Clem Cattini played this on hundreds of sessions with The Kinks, Tom Jones and many others.

Beck Bogert & Appice sleeve (left) After playing with Vanilla Fudge, Carmine Appice joined up with Jeff Beck and bassist Tim Bogert in 1973.

Carmine Appice c1973 (above) Around 1968 Appice pioneered heavy rock drumming using oversize drums, which would influence John Bonham. He has also written successful songs (such as 'Do Ya Think I'm Sexy' for Rod Stewart). Here Appice can be seen using Ludwig Octaplus single-headed 'melodic' toms as well as a Supraphonic 400 snare drum.

36

Johnny Kidd & The Pirates
(right) The first time drummer Clem
Cattini entered a recording studio the
result was a number one hit for Kidd &
the Pirates with 'Shakin' All Over'
(1960). When Cattini left to work with
The Tornados (inset, right) his place in
the Pirates was taken by Frank 'The
Animal' Farley (main pic, with Ludwig
400 snare), another legend of the early
British rock scene. With The Tornados –
house band of "Britain's Phil Spector",
Joe Meek – drummer/leader Cattini
had a number one hit in Britain (1962)
and the US (1963) with Meek's
instrumental composition 'Telstar'.

37

**Ludwig Speedking bass drum
pedal** (below) Several improvements
were made at the start of the 1950s to
the original 1937 Speedking, including
a wider footplate and an arched rocker
shaft for extra foot clearance. With the
unusual concealed springs, which are
compressed rather than stretched, and
the reversible split or one-piece
footboard, the Speedking became
probably the most popular pedal ever.

Kula Shaker 1996 (above)
Many new British bands during
the 1990s have paid homage to
the guitar-group music of the
1960s and 1970s, confidently
revitalising the genre, and

the fashion has extended to the use of
vintage instruments. Paul Winterhart of
Kula Shaker plays an early 1970s
Slingerland kit in Sparkling Silver
Pearl with various Ludwig
snare drums.

THE RHYTHM SECTION

American drums remained more expensive, beyond the reach of the average British basher. The Hollies' Bobby Elliott, easily the classiest of the first wave of Northern beat group drummers, appeared in ads stating that he could afford any make of drums and he chose Premier. But Elliott eventually got frustrated with Premier. When Elliott visited Ludwig in Chicago in 1968 he jumped at the chance to swap his Premier kit for a blue glitter Super Classic.

One stumbling block that many drummers of the time mention was Premier's refusal to produce a tom in the popular 9x13 size, instead sticking to their 8x14. The problem with the 8x14 tom was probably not so much the diameter as the depth, which was the same as for the 12″ tom. Deeper 10x14 and 12x14 drums were around in the 1940s, and have since returned to prove once more how well they work.

BITS AND PIECES

Ludwig opened the door in Britain for the other major American drum manufacturers, Gretsch and Slingerland. However, the most conspicuous American brand besides Ludwig in early-1960s Britain was Rogers. This was for two reasons. First, Buddy Rich finished a long association with Ludwig and from 1960 to 1966 was a Rogers endorser. Although Rich was a jazz drummer who couldn't resist knocking the young rockers, his self-styled reputation as the world's greatest drummer and his superhuman dedication to proving it inspired total awe in most rock drummers.

The second reason couldn't have been in greater contrast. For a brief period in 1964 The Dave Clark Five was the first group to be lumbered with that kiss of death title, Bigger Than The Beatles. Dave Clark played Rogers, and a particularly distinctive Rogers kit at that. It was red glitter, and had two mounted tom toms – virtually unique in Britain at the time. Clark was also a natural self publicist, a drummer-leader who sat out front of his group with a perfect toothpaste-ad smile as he pounded his kit in a fashion not seen before or since.

Rogers had been around for years but Rich's endorsement coincided with the company's elevation to that of a major drum innovator. Rogers became the most highly regarded maker of the most expensive American drums. The company had opened the modern era of hardware design with their catchily named Swiv-O-Matic tom holders, pedals and stands which appeared in 1957, the work of design engineer Joe Thompson. This was the hardware innovation that the drum kit had long awaited, and created the bridge from the lightweight designs of the jazz years to the heavy duty hardware of the rock era. It was a revelation.

The Swiv-O-Matic system increased flexibility and stability by the use of a ball-and-clamp device. The ball was, ingeniously, egg-shaped so that it was pushed down into its socket and secured using a drum key. Hexagonal hardened-steel mounting rods prevented any chance of slippage. As testament to its popularity many drummers, including Keith Moon of The Who and Dennis Wilson of The Beach Boys, fitted Swiv-O-Matic hardware onto their kits of other makes.

The Rogers make-over also included a classic snare drum, the Dyna-Sonic, reputedly designed for Rich. This had a flanged-for-strength chromed brass shell and a bulky aluminium frame suspended beneath which enclosed the snares at full tension without choking the bottom head. When the final weak link with Rogers' drums was eliminated – the cast 'beavertail' lugs replacing the easily cracked drawn-brass 'bread and butter' lugs – you had one hell of a drum kit, arguably the finest contemporary example of the American drum maker's craft.

The far reaching importance of Swiv-O-Matic hardware is best illustrated by the way Pearl copied it in the 1970s before changing to their present system, while to this day Tama, Yamaha and Mapex tom tom mounts are basically enlarged versions of the Swiv-O-Matic concept, using resinated balls and hexagonal rods.

ENGLISH ROGERS

While Rogers wowed the Americans they were held back in Britain because of a most unusual situation. A special British-version Rogers kit was made which consisted of, at first, imported Rogers fittings mounted onto Ajax shells. The Ajax shells were no match for the five-ply maple shells of the American Rogers, but the arrangement presumably allowed the drums to be sold at a realistic price, perhaps even more so when the Swiv-O-Matic fittings were later produced in Britain (albeit with slightly different proportions that made them incompatible with the American originals).

Before the Ajax name disappeared completely in 1970 there

was a final attempt to update their image with the introduction of the Nu Sound line in 1967. Ironically these drums should have taken over from the English Rogers, and looked not unlike the earlier Rogers which had suffered from the poor lug design. Out went the Ajax cast rims and lugs to be replaced by triple-flange rims. New pressed lugs with 'A's stamped on them suffered similar design failings to the earlier Rogers lugs. Unfortunately, the Ajax didn't really stand much of a chance. It was a handsome kit, but it was too little too late.

THE DERANGED SYMPHONY

The speed at which the music developed in the 1960s is astounding. From the beginning of 1963 when the Beatles had their first hit it was just four years before audiences were wowed by Cream and Jimi Hendrix – a quantum leap in terms of instrumental virtuosity. The jump from the beat era of the Liverpool groups to the rock era of loud bands was personified by The Who. Keith Moon was the major figure in the mid-1960s British change from innocent, cheeky beat music to anarchic, outrageous rock. No one since, including the vilest of the punks and the coarsest of the heavy metal hordes, has come close to displacing him as the embodiment of the wild drummer. The down side, ironically, is that probably no one's done more to harm the drummer's image.

The Who were a pop group with loads of hit singles, and yet their approach to musical arrangement was more adventurous from the start. This had a lot to do with Moon's abandoned onslaught of the kit, egged on by Pete Townshend's circular strumming and experiments with feedback. Moon showed how the drums in rock didn't always have to follow a repetitive, unchanging beat – no, the drums could be hugely dynamic like the kettledrums in a deranged symphony, ranging from a scary whisper to full blown chaos.

Although The Who took things to extremes, much of the platform for their improvisations came from the typical British band's love of jamming for hours on the riffs of old blues standards. The masters at this were Eric Clapton, Jack Bruce and Ginger Baker, who came together in Cream to take rock improvisation to an intensity which no one before had suspected possible. Baker invested in rock drumming a new level of virtuosity and power. With his tom toms and twin bass drums he conjured up an African tribal feel which was

shocking for the time. And close on Baker's heels was Mitch Mitchell, encouraged and inspired beyond his wildest dreams by the great Jimi Hendrix. Somehow Mitchell managed to conjure totally sympathetic song accompaniment, interspersed with wonderfully inventive musical fills, and again rounded out with free-form, bluesy jamming.

EXTENDING THE KIT

As drummers extended the scope of rock it was just a matter of time before the drum kit itself underwent change. The alterations were small at first. The four-piece kit was extended to a five-piece by adding an extra floor tom or mounted tom. This was not a new idea, but it became commonplace. Jerry Allison with Buddy Holly had gone so far as to use four toms in the 1950s when most country drummers didn't have any.

By the late 1960s double mounted-toms became standard, although at first the two mounted toms were the same size. Later, the obvious advantage of having a 12″ and a 13″ drum on the kit clicked. Once it did the line-up of the standard kit went from four-piece to five-piece, and this has remained the norm to the present day, with a line-up of 22″ bass, 12″, 13″ and 16″ toms, plus a 5x14 snare.

As this was happening a small number of rock drummers started to experiment with double bass drum kits. These were at first assembled from two separate kits brought together, giving paired drums of each size and type. Double bass drum kits had debuted many years earlier, the most famous example being Louie Bellson's mammoth multi-tom Gretsch kit of 1947. But in rock it was Ginger Baker who led the way with his double silver sparkle Ludwigs, also copying Bellson's earlier use of double tiered cymbals. Baker had his kit customised to include a 20″ and a 22″ bass drum, one of them cut down to 11″ deep. This delay actually enabled Keith Moon to get his first double Premier kit two weeks before Baker's was ready. Towards the end of the 1960s Nick Mason of Pink Floyd also used a double kit, moving from Premier to Ludwig, and Mitch Mitchell appeared with Hendrix at the 1970 Isle of Wight Festival with a double set of black Gretsch drums.

The Baker-inspired set-up appeared in Ludwig's 1973 catalogue as the Rock Duo, with a special double stand to mount 9x13 and 10x14 toms between twin 22″ bass drums. The problem of what to do with the hi-hat was in fact temporarily

39

Gretsch catalogue (right) In the 1940s the American Gretsch company pioneered staggered plywood shells without reinforcing hoops, followed by smaller drums which won them great support with small-group jazz drummers. Today in the 1990s it's not just the jazzers, but — as the cliché goes — almost every rock drummer who has a Gretsch at home or plays one in the studio. Gretsch's maple shells and heavy die-cast rims have remained unchanged for years. Perhaps that's the secret?

Hand-finished
for the head, heart and gut of a drummer:
Anatomy of a legend in its second hundred years.

Charlie Watts' Gretsch kit (right; see also front, opposite) Watts has endorsed Gretsch since 1968. This is his much-loved Rolling Stones kit, normally set on a red carpet. It's a 1957 'round badge' Gretsch, plus Rogers Swiv-O-Matic hi-hat and Ludwig Speedking pedal (with heel-plate reversed).

Phil Collins (right) Collins' success as a vocalist/writer has over-shadowed his love of drums; his input to the quasi-classical arrangements of early Genesis, for example, was invaluable. Collins has long endorsed Gretsch, staying with single-headed toms long after most players had reverted to double heads.

Charlie Watts' Gretsch kit (front, above) Charlie's 1957 kit comprises natural maple 14x22, 8x12 and 16x16 toms, with a (recent) 8x14 Pearl MLX maple-shell ten-lug snare drum. The Gretsch telescopic spurs are original, the small tom is mounted on a snare drum stand, and the four cymbal stands are Gretsch Techwares. Cymbals are two Ufip Experience 18" Chinas (one with 12 rivets), an Arbiter Custom (Paiste) Formula 602, un-named Italian 18" flat ride, and 14" Avedis Zildjian hi-hats. Heads are Remo CS Black Dots on top and bottom of toms, a coated Remo Ambassador snare batter, and a clear Evans Hydraulic bass drum batter with a clear Gretsch cut-out on front.

41

Charlie Watts (above) Watts is living proof that you can drive "the world's greatest rock band" with nonchalant ease, partly due to the jazzy snap of his traditional-grip fat backbeat. His importance to the Stones was emphasised back in 1970 when he made a rare solo appearance on the cover of the band's raucous live album, Get Yer Ya Yas Out (inset left).

solved by closing up the tripod, and then clamping the hi-hat to the rim of the left bass drum by means of a hi-hat 'brace'.

BACK IN AMERICA

Britain in the 1960s had seen not only a great revolution in pop music, but also – at last – the best of American drum gear. Of course, there was nothing new about Ludwig and the rest in the US. Andy Newmark, who grew up in the New York area, says: "My first kit was a Gretsch. It seemed great then, but today I might think it was flimsy – who knows? I started around 1962 and the gear at the time was Gretsch, Ludwig, Slingerland and Rogers. I only heard of Leedy later, and it was vintage to me – you never saw any."

To this list we should add one other name, that of Camco. Camco are the least well known of all the 1960s American drums, which is a pity because they have a great pedigree. They resulted from drum guru George Way's shortlived attempt to manufacture drums under his own name during the middle 1950s, which he did, only to lose the company to Camco in 1962. The most notable Camco rock endorser was Dennis Wilson of The Beach Boys. The drums, with their distinctive turret lugs and quality maple shells, disappeared at the end of the 1970s. But the legacy of George Way and Camco would in fact give rise to two important modern companies, namely Drum Workshop and Ayotte.

Because of the unique success of the British drummers who followed Ringo, the importance of the American drummers of the 1960s was for once overshadowed. I asked Andy Newmark who were his American heroes. "I was into Dino Danelli of the Rascals, he was the Buddy Rich of rock'n'roll. He had chops and a lot of soul, and was very visual, with a fantastic vibe. Dino was the opposite of Ringo and Charlie Watts, he had lots of left-hand stuff going, and did the James Brown 'Cold Sweat' type beats, not just the back beat. He played really funky for the time," says Newmark.

The stick-twirling Danelli has cited Count Basie's Sonny Payne as his main inspiration for showmanship. Danelli made the first Rascals LP on a red sparkle Rogers with a 24″ bass drum, but he's generally known for playing several highly distinctive Ludwig kits. One was silver sparkle with horizontal black stripes through the middle of each drum. He also mounted his 9x13 tom on a snare stand, which was one

solution to the problem of the feeble tom brackets of the day. Charlie Watts, who plays a Gretsch kit from the 1950s, still does this, as do many other players.

After The Beatles it became the perceived norm for groups to write their own material and perform it on record. Of course the truth is that session musicians were still employed on pop recordings more often than was realised or admitted. Andy Newmark says, "When you're 14 you don't know the names, you hear the music. I had the greatest hits of Chuck Berry but I didn't know who the players were. I had Otis Redding, and Sam & Dave, and so I was into [drummer] Al Jackson although I didn't know his name. By 17 or 18 I was hearing specific players, and went to see James Brown live once, but before 1965 they didn't credit players. Hal Blaine on The Mamas & The Papas records is maybe the first credit I know of."

Hal Blaine was the LA-based session drummer who played on hit records by The Beach Boys ('Good Vibrations'), The Mamas & The Papas ('California Dreaming'), The Byrds ('Mr Tambourine Man'), and Sonny & Cher ('I Got You Babe'), as well as a thousand others – more than anyone else throughout the 1960s and 1970s. Blaine played Ludwig for the most part and, coming from the old school, always used a calf head on his bass drum.

The other unsung session heroes of the 1960s were the drummers of Motown. Ricky Lawson, who grew up in Detroit and today plays for Michael Jackson and Steely Dan, was lucky enough to see these players live. "My uncle is Paul Riser, one of the arrangers for Motown," says Lawson. "So as a youngster he'd take me along and I'd sit and watch [drummers] Uriel Jones, Benny Benjamin and Marvin Gaye. They were my first influences, and they played in the clubs like The Twenty Grand, and The Motown Review down at the Fox Theatre. They were playing Ludwig and Rogers."

The Motown drummers and Al Jackson were also a major influence on British rock drummers. Jackson was a technically accomplished player who had the priceless knack of playing for the song. He defined the coolness of simplicity and a rock solid groove with the result that 30 years later everyone still dances to those old Stax soul hits. There are many photographs of Jackson playing a Ludwig Super Classic with metal 5″ Supraphonic snare, but apparently in the studio he used a wood shell Rogers Powertone.

HAYMAN, WHAT'S HAPPENING?

In 1968 Ivor Arbiter decided to put the experiences he'd gained with Trixon and Ludwig into making a British drum. He became involved with one of the oldest drum making companies in Britain, John E Dallas, whose Carlton drum factory "was losing a fortune" according to Arbiter. Gerry Evans was enlisted and taken along to look at the factory. "I'd never seen anything like it," says Evans. "It was like the 1930s – Heath Robinson with gas pipes and copper tubing. They were steam-bending plywood, which they were good at. So Ivor said, 'We're going to turn this into a modern factory, and I've had a great idea, we're going to take these Carlton shells and line them with brass.'"

Arbiter explains: "I'd learned so much about drums and drummers I thought I must have a go. I wanted to produce a British kit which sounded as good as the Americans. I started messing with an idea with Paiste funnily enough, a prototype kit with wood shells lined with brass. I carted these things to Switzerland. They weighed a ton. We did some soundchecks and it was terrible. Then I realised, having had a lot of experience with saxes and clarinets, that all we needed was a hard lining – and that it didn't have to be metal. That's when we sprayed the interior with four or five coats of polyurethane. A guy called Gerry Waller, who'd been at Premier, came to us and developed the shells."

Arbiter was able to hear the positive results in his nightclub, Caesar's Palace in Luton, with big band drummer Alf Bigden playing for Shirley Bassey in front of 1500 people. "And we didn't mike up in those days," he points out.

The new drums were called George Hayman, later shortened to Hayman. Arbiter: "At Dallas there was a shell maker who was about 70 years old named George Haymon, and I thought, 'That sounds like a great American teacher.' We built this big mystique about George. But it was the first British product that sounded right and looked right. We got right away from the orthodox pearl finishes."

Evans claims to have found Hayman's striking finishes at a plastics exhibition where he came upon a bright metallic covering which was conventionally used mostly for nameplates on refrigerators and music systems. The Hayman finishes were in place. "But we still had the bullet shape nut boxes," says Evans. "So I'd had a George Way kit in 1963 and I thought, why

not do the Way circular nut box? The tool guy said that would be easier to make than anything. So they started to make them by hand: the early ones are individually turned and very heavy. The later ones were lighter. Also, we made a simple Ludwig type snare release and spurs, and the tool shop came out with a tom holder that was a work of art."

One mock-up gold kit was made, according to Evans, who toured Britain for six weeks selling the new kit to music stores. "I rang Ivor at the end of each week and gave the orders: Luton two, Rochdale one... it was like the football results. I came back and I'd sold about 150 kits, and I'd quoted six weeks delivery to all of them. So then Ivor phoned the factory and said, 'Let's go ahead and make 50 kits.' It took five months, and even that was quite quick. Eventually they got them in September 1968."

Hayman took the British market by storm with their fresh, modern look, totally unlike any previous British drums. The sound was bright and loud, the shells were quite thin three-ply mahogany with reinforcing glue rings, and the 'Vibrasonic' lining of thick white paint was a better interior finish than Ludwig's. The snare drums had a shallow snare bed which Arbiter says was important to the sound. If anything let them down it was the tom tom holder which was strong... but a real knuckle cruncher. Later on, Hayman stands and pedals were also produced. Cosmetically the turret lugs made the drums look very similar to Camco, though few were aware of the resemblance at the time.

Hayman was very successful for a while in the early 1970s. Simon Kirke played a silver Hayman with Free, and Richard Bailey recorded Jeff Beck's classic *Blow By Blow* album on Hayman (with a Rogers Dynasonic snare). Nicko McBrain, now with Iron Maiden, had a nine-piece Hayman kit in his earlier years.

Unfortunately the Dallas-Arbiter partnership did not last. Dallas held on to the drums, but went broke in about 1975... and that was the end of Hayman.

NATURAL PROGRESSION

Rock music took off and became enormously popular during the 1960s. By the end of the decade it seemed anything was possible. The cream of young British musical talent had been so inspired by The Beatles that many who in previous generations would have become jazz or classical players put

43

Premier 1970s bass drum heads (below) The advantage of keeping the front head intact was that drummers could indulge in the colourful practice of personalised painted heads.

Kenney Jones 1974 (right) During the mid 1970s Rod Stewart and The Faces built up a fanatical following of tartan-wearing fans. Drummer Kenney Jones asked Premier to make a Kenny Clare Resonator kit finished in Royal Stewart tartan. The bare wood shells were covered in material used for real kilts which was then protected by transparent acetate.

Keith Moon's endorsement letter (below) This is Moon's original agreement with Premier, signed over a sixpenny stamp on September 6th 1965 and lasting three years. It affords the lowly drummer little, while Premier holds all the trump cards. Previously, top endorsers had been jazz stars. Moon stayed with Premier, although he did play Gretsch wood snare drums.

Keith Moon's custom Premier 'Pictures Of Lily' kit 1968 (above) The first and most memorable of Keith Moon's customised Premier kits started when Moon asked Premier for a kit with then-fashionable 'pop art' designs. Premier set to work with Jeff Hurst from the company's advertising agency, Cunningham-Hurst. Moon himself suggested including 'Lily' from artwork that had been used for The Who's single 'Pictures Of Lily'. In the end the job was rushed as the group's 1968 US tour was brought forward by two weeks, and the kit had to be completed with a deadline of July 5th 1968. The fluorescent designs were applied to standard Premier shells using a form of decoupage, with the pictures mounted onto the shell and covered in clear acetate. (Note that the bass drums are held together by Gretsch fittings, while the tom mounts are actually Rogers Swiv-O-Matics.)

Keith Moon (below) Roadies would have spare snares ready on the top of stands, because the base was nailed to the floor. They'd dive in and throw out the old top for a colleague to catch.

Keith Moon's Premier White and Copper kit (above and right) Premier's Roger Horrobin remembers that Keith wanted a white and gold kit, but when he worked out the cost of the gold and the insurance he decided to go with copper. Moon gave the kit to Ringo, who passed it to his son Zak Starkey, Keith's biggest fan, and most recently drumming with The Who Quadrophenia show. The kit reflects the early 1970s period, with an extra six single-headed toms added to the Lily set-up (note also the Gretsch snare drum, right). For touring, Moon's kit was reinforced by steel frames inside the bass drums supporting the first row of 14" double-headed toms — sometimes he'd stand on the top and walk over the front. Moon's roadie Mick Double ('Doc') kept a travelling workshop of hardened steel plates.

their energies into rock. The result was that every kind of music was fair game.

Folk music went electric, while elements of Indian, jazz and classical music were plundered. The straight eighths pulse which now pervaded most rock music was easily extended into the odd time signatures of European classical and folk musics. This gave rise to bands like King Crimson, Emerson Lake & Palmer (ELP) and Yes, whose music was given the general label of 'progressive' rock.

In cynical old Britain progressive rock now suggests something overblown and pompous, but at the time this was not the way it was seen at all. At the start of the 1970s no one knew how far rock could go, and there was a naively optimistic determination to stretch the boundaries. The British bands felt an almost moral obligation to reciprocate the gift of largely black American music which had so inspired them, by offering up their European legacy. Included in this was the use of classical percussion. Carl Palmer in Emerson Lake & Palmer assembled an incredible array complete with tuned percussion, timpani and gongs, the like of which had last been seen way back in the days of Sonny Greer and Duke Ellington.

From Bonham to Cobham

Around the same time, the 'blues boom' in Britain graduated into heavy metal through bands like Deep Purple, Black Sabbath and Led Zeppelin, spurred on by America's Vanilla Fudge and Iron Butterfly. They too felt it natural to extend the blues, this time with their European gothic black humour. The heavy boys – following the example set by Fudge's Carmine Appice – started to use outsize drums. John Bonham had a 26″ bass drum with 12x15 mounted tom, 16″ and 18″ floor toms and the deeper (6½″) 402 Supraphonic snare replacing the standard 400. But Bonham, while laying down the blueprint for heavy drumming, was never just a basher. His unmistakably deep groove and huge sound still command awe and bewilderment; he gave to rock drumming what today we'd probably describe as 'attitude'.

So the bad boys went for HM, the college boys went for prog rock and the jazzers went for, well... jazz-rock fusion. Spearheaded by the jazz trumpeter Miles Davis, who'd discovered a brilliant young drummer in Tony Williams, jazz musicians started to play straight eighth rhythms – and a

whole new area opened up. Miles' protégé, the guitarist John McLaughlin, formed the Mahavishnu Orchestra in 1971 and coaxed the jazz drummer Billy Cobham into playing double bass drums the following year. Cobham went for it big time. He built a double bass drum kit with multiple toms, and re-introduced ideas from earlier decades, including a mounted gong drum (made by cutting a 22″ bass drum shell in half) with an oversize 24″ timpani head fitted to it. He also took a 22″ Swish China cymbal minus the rivets, mounted it upside down and high up, and trashed it for a scary ride effect, something like a giant's half open hi-hat.

The end of the 1960s saw rock groups playing massive outdoor concerts with audiences of tens of thousands. The 30 watt amps of the early 1960s were clearly inadequate, and Jim Marshall (himself a drummer) set the pattern with his 50 watt amp stacks, which quickly became 100 watts, and then multiplied in power according to the Law Of Spinal Tap.

Soon the rock drummer found himself in the historically novel situation of not being able to make himself heard – there's a nice irony! I twice witnessed the heart-rending sight of Mitch Mitchell vainly giving his all, only to be drowned out by Jimi and bassist Noel Redding. There might have been an overhead mike or two, but close miking wasn't here yet. So while the PA companies and mike people got their act together, drum manufacturers turned to making shells with synthetic materials which, it was hoped, would be louder and maybe stronger than wood.

See-through Ginger

In an era when inlaid mahogany parlour pianos were chopped up and passed through hoops during charity fund-raising events, the idea of producing synthetic drum shells seemed wholly appropriate. In fact – in keeping with the times – the idea was to make everything, including drums, from plastic.

Amazingly, Ginger Baker may well be the first person ever to have made a Perspex (Plexiglas) kit – in 1961. He did this by cutting out squares of Perspex and bending them over his gas stove to form shells. He played the kit from 1961 to 1966, even using it to record the classic Graham Bond Organisation albums *Sound Of '65* and *There's A Bond Between Us* (both 1965) before he got his first wood-shell Ludwigs. Later in the 1970s Baker had the satisfaction of playing a see-through

Mitch Mitchell 1967 (right)
Mitchell was a London session musician when he and bassist Noel Redding were enlisted into The Jimi Hendrix Experience in 1966. Until the group split in 1969 they produced three albums of unsurpassed originality. The first, Are You Experienced (1967, left), might be the greatest rock album ever – and Mitchell (on the left) was just a boy. It seems he was born to play with Hendrix, his pushy triplet rolls being the perfect match for Jimi's swooping feedback. When it came to Hendrix's more considered songs, Mitchell dreamed up some of the most musical and apt fills ever heard in rock. Mitchell is seen (right) playing a Ludwig Super Classic, the definitive rock drum kit, but he also played Premier and Gretsch kits at various times with Hendrix.

Ginger Baker (left) Baker was the chief instigator in rock of the double-bass-drum extended kit. He also elevated the drum solo from a Sandy Nelson-style novelty item into the heavier area of African-inspired poly-rhythms. His tom and bass drum ostinati are alive today in the amazing solos of Terry Bozzio and Dennis Chambers. Baker and bassist Jack Bruce played in the seminal jazz-rock outfit The Graham Bond Organisation before teaming up with guitarist Eric Clapton in Cream. Baker has always favoured Ludwig drums, though he often played a Leedy snare drum with his famous silver glitter Ludwig kit (pictured left) which had 20" and 22" bass drums.

HAYMAN

Hayman (left) A youthful Ivor Arbiter (far left, top) proudly shows off his Hayman products in the 1971 brochure, which included top British rock and jazz endorsers such as Aynsley Dunbar (far left, bottom) and Rob Townsend (main picture, left). Dunbar is probably the most underrated British rock drummer of the late 1960s, with a bass foot as fleet as Bonham's. He was a revelation with John Mayall's Bluesbreakers (Hard Road, 1967) and in the original Jeff Beck Group. Frank Zappa invited him to LA where he joined The Mothers Of Invention, subsequently recording eight albums. He later played with Jefferson Starship and helped form Journey. Rob Townsend of Family, whose influential 1969 album Entertainment (inset) reached number 6 in the UK, played this Hayman Big Sound with 15x26 bass drum. Note the classic use of a huge stage weight to anchor the bass drum.

Cream sleeve (left) Cream's double-album Wheels Of Fire of 1968 had one disc recorded in the studio and the other live at The Fillmore, the latter half including a 15-minute rendition of Baker's famed drum solo, 'Toad'.

Hayman Vibrasonic 5½x14 wood snare drum in Regal Red (right) Hayman drums were made from 1968-1975, aiming to leapfrog Premier and make a British drum along more fashionable American lines. Thus the shells had a white painted interior like Ludwig and others, but Hayman's Vibrasonic multi-coat polyurethane lining was opaque. The drums produced a bright almost metallic timbre. The snare drum also had ten Camco-style lugs, triple-flanged rims, and straightforward Ludwig P83-type strainer. Previously, European drums had mostly die-cast lugs and rims.

Hayman Showman kit (above)
Trevor Morais pounds a Showman five-piece which has the murderous, bone-crunching double-tom mount. Ouch!

Rob Townsend (Family)   Blue   26" Big Sound Kit

John Bonham (right) Here Bonham plays his Ludwig Amber Vistalite kit with 26" bass drum and paired 16" and 18" floor toms, plus large Paiste gong. The same kit (below) was auctioned recently by Philips. Bonham was loyal to Ludwig, playing a maple kit and a stainless steel kit before and after the Vistalites, usually with the larger 12x15 mounted tom and a chrome 6.5" Supra-phonic 402. Bonham used Paiste Giant Beat cymbals, and later 2002s, sometimes including a 24" ride along with 16" and 18" crashes, plus 15" Sound Edge hi-hats. Bonham is probably Britain's most imitated drummer, due to his pivotal role in the development of heavy rock with Led Zeppelin. His sound was big rather than simply loud, and still fascinates and puzzles drummers. Part of the secret lies in the band's soulful approach (Bonham was influenced as much by Al Jackson and Bernard Purdie as by Buddy Rich) and the way Bonham was always striving for a subtlety of groove — something that escapes most heavy rockers.

NO. 2201 CLEAR NO. 2205 YELLOW NO. 2208 AMBER

NO. 2236 RED NO. 2216 BLUE NO. 2241 GREEN

Ludwig Vistalite snares, early 1970s (above) Plexiglas Vistalites were made in various colours. Kits were also produced in Rainbow stripes, culminating in the Tivoli with tiny 'space age' lights inside.

1975 IVOR ARBITER INVENTED AUTOTUNE PERCUSSION FEATURING INSTANT TUNING WITH A BIGGER SOUND

Arbiter Autotune Outfit
Pure White Rock No. 100

A MAJOR CONTRIBUTION TO THE PERCUSSIVE ART

Arbiter Autotune catalogue
1975 (left) Following his success with Hayman, Ivor Arbiter tried his hand at a more experimental design. He reasoned that it's impossible to tune conventional drums accurately: "You tighten one lug and it loosens another," he says. "You're chasing yourself. It's so antiquated, with all the money going on expensive nuts and bolts." So Autotune drums used the 'pickle jar' principle of screwing the head down evenly. Jon Hiseman and Carl Palmer helped in the development. However, Arbiter didn't reckon on the average drummer's conservatism. Plus, the original Autotunes (like the Pure White Outfit 100 shown in this catalogue, left) had fibreglass shells, which Arbiter says proved "too heavy, expensive and difficult to mould accurately". Later Autotunes were made from wood with the interiors sprayed like Hayman.

Hayman Iceberg kit, early 1970s (above) Hayman drums were popular in Britain from 1968 into the mid 1970s. A few were made in Plexiglas like this clear Iceberg Showman five-piece kit.

Carl Palmer's stainless steel kit c1975 (above) Palmer used this custom-made kit live and in the studio with ELP (including the Brain Salad Surgery album). Rims are Gretsch, with custom rose-shaped copper lugs. The engravings, from field mice on the 6" drum to a horse and cart on the 18", are by jeweller Paul Raven, inspired by British gun maker Purdey. The two consoles also supported cymbal arms, snare cradle and microphones.

Ludwig Vistalite when commercially-produced Plexiglas shells became familiar. The most famous see-through kits were Billy Cobham's Fibes acrylic Crystalite kit (with mostly Slingerland hardware) and John Bonham's orange Ludwig Vistalite, which was similar to Baker's. Probably the earliest success in America was the Zickos kit played by Iron Butterfly's drummer Ron Bushy, immortalised by his solo on the band's anthemic 'In-A-Gadda-Da-Vida' (1968).

Before long just about every company had a go at plastics. For example, Wishbone Ash drummer Steve Upton had a see-through French kit made by Orange (Capelle), and the Japanese company Pearl had its Crystal Beat. Keith Moon just had to have a see-through kit – and, being Keith, famously filled it with water and fish before a live American TV appearance, causing great waves of disgust among the animal welfare lobby.

Ludwig Vistalites were available in yellow, blue, amber, red and green, and in fantastic colour combinations called Swirls and Rainbows. The ultimate was Ludwig's 1979 Tivoli which had rows of tiny space-age lights set into the plastic: "The lights that light space capsules at night are the same lights that will amaze audiences," ran the blurb. Not that lights inside drums was a new idea – oh no. Yet again, they had been common earlier in the century.

THE FAT ALPINE HORN

The other material exploited in the 1970s was fibreglass. Fibreglass is strong, impervious to moisture, and can be moulded into shapes which would be impossible for conventional wood (mind you, don't tell Mr Trixon that). The leading company was Fibes who started out in 1966 and took a great deal of care in compression-moulding the fibreglass. The result was drums that were expensive but of high quality. The shells were mostly covered in metallic plastics and had distinctive diamond lugs which later (after 1979) appeared on Corder, and then on Darwin wood drums. However, Fibes Crystalite kits and fibreglass snare drums have, at the time of writing, just become available once more.

After Fibes came two of the weirdest looking drums ever, the American North, designed by Roger North, and the British Staccato, designed by Pat Townsend. North produced his drums from 1972 and among his first customers were Billy Cobham, who added a couple to the outside edges of his acrylic Fibes kit, Doug 'Cosmo' Clifford of Creedence Clearwater Revival, and Gerry Brown (Lionel Richie, Stevie Wonder) who had a flame-painted North kit. The North tom tom shape was a cylinder which curved so that the bottom end was facing towards the audience, projecting the sound directly forward – like a fat alpine horn.

Pat Townsend's design for Staccato was more convoluted, inspired by a painting he'd done of a tree. Staccato drums also curved forward, but the bass drum was a doubled shape, like a huge pair of trouser legs. The toms, however, always reminded me, from the front, of the shape of Batman's cape. Staccato debuted in 1977 at The Golden Lion, a pub venue in west London, where they were played by Mitch Mitchell. They were marketed through Bob Henrit's Drum Store in Wardour Street and were used briefly by many drummers such as Keith Moon, John Bonham, Simon Phillips (Jeff Beck, The Who) and Nicko McBrain. Staccato drums have recently been produced by the Canadian drum company Ayotte.

Following the Hayman experience, Ivor Arbiter decided to tread a more experimental path with Autotune, which were fibreglass drums incorporating a revolutionary tuning method. Arbiter explains: "I had this thing that tuning drums is so antiquated, with all the money going on expensive lugs and bolts. You can never tune a drum accurately: you tighten one lug and it loosens another. You're chasing yourself. So, I was in the kitchen and I looked at my wife's pressure cooker, and I thought, 'Why don't we pull the counter hoop down evenly?' I also had a thing about sound, which is why we started off with fibreglass. That was a big mistake, actually, because you can't mould it accurately enough. It's expensive and it's heavy. We eventually went to wood."

With the Arbiter Autotune kit, tuning was accomplished by turning a single bolt. This meant that the shells had smooth lines. "One thing we found that was against it was the appearance," Arbiter continues. "I thought it looked wonderful, but the kids didn't. It was too bland without lugs."

Steel is often used in making snare drum shells and it's also been used from time to time for whole kits, resulting in a loud, reverberant sound. John Bonham, for example, played a stainless-steel Ludwig. But the most impressive steel kit was the magnificent stainless engraved set made for Carl Palmer with

ELP around 1975. Wouldn't you just love to have been Carl's roadie? Carl also had a steel kit made by Premier in the late 1970s. At this time Premier made chrome-plated wood-shell drums. Chrome finishes were also seen on Slingerland, Ludwig, Gretsch and Pearl drums, while Slingerland also did a beautiful copper finish kit.

Throughout the 1970s, live and studio engineers developed techniques of 'close miking', which put drum sounds under closer scrutiny than ever before. Volume by itself was not enough and the fashion for synthetic shells waned. Simultaneously the economies of the West came under intense pressure, making plastics and steel expensive. Add to this fears about the damage to lungs caused by working with fibreglass and the upshot was that the drum world reverted to wood. However, fibreglass was successfully used by Pearl (both fibreglass and a wood-fibreglass mixture), and several companies including Impact, Milestone and Tempus have since persevered with it. There's even been a brightly coloured fibreglass drum head, called Canasonic.

Tom Loses His Head

Single-headed tom toms returned in the early 1970s. Hal Blaine, the leading West Coast session drummer, augmented his standard four-piece kit with a pair of metal timbales. These were of course single-headed, and produced a more incisive, one-dimensional sound than his usual double-headed toms... which got him to thinking about using a whole row of them.

At the same time, multitrack recording and close miking of each part of the drum kit exposed the sound of every drum to a merciless scrutiny, magnifying every rattle and overtone. Horrified studio and live engineers took to damping down drum heads with tape in order to get a clean signal. An easy solution to the problem was to remove the bottom heads, since single heads produce fewer overtones.

Before anyone had much time to think about it, single-headed drums were in fashion. Previously, single-headed drums signalled 'cheap' or 'starter'. Now they were marketed as 'concert' toms or 'melodic' toms, since whole rows of them could be tuned to exact intervals.

The Ludwig Octaplus was a set of eight melodic toms: 6″, 8″, 10″, 12″, 13″, 14″, 15″ and 16″. Reflecting Hal Blaine's original inspiration, they were mounted on new timbale-type

Sturdi-lok floor stands or tom mounts. Ludwig, as tuned percussion experts, took this very seriously. The toms were lined with a hard maple veneer for greater projection, and particular weights of Ludwig heads were specified. The bigger toms – 13″ through to 16″ – had a special circular-patterned treatment on the underside of each head to give more 'tonal centre'.

Soon, every company made toms in single-headed as well as double-headed versions. Most drummers with double headed kits simply removed the bottom heads and rims. At this stage the front head came off the bass drum too, a mike was inserted right inside, and serious amounts of damping became normal. One of Britain's busiest rock session drummers was Clem Cattini. "I was the first British drummer to take the front head off," Cattini claims. "I was watching a TV show from America and noticed the drummer had done it, so I thought I'd give it a try.

"Also, purely by luck, I was the first to get that 'duuoom' dropping tom tom sound. I used to wallop shit out of the kit, and one of the tension rods got loose, making that sound. The engineer heard it and said, 'Keep it like that, it sounds great.' Then everyone started to get it." What came next was the heavily damped 'cardboard' tom sound of the 1970s. "It went nuts after that," says Cattini, who continues: "I've had tape, cigarette packets, newspapers, everything stuck to the top head for dampening. I hated that 'breadboard' sound, with all the resonance taken out."

All Change at Ludwig

The rock world had grown into an international stadium-filling business and the drum kit had to withstand the increasing rigours of touring and a new intensity of playing. Big, hairy rockers kept breaking things – heads, sticks, cymbals, hardware, even shells.

After flirting with synthetics, the manufacturers largely returned to wood. But now they wondered if the shells were strong enough. The traditional American drum shell had been relatively thin: the Ludwig shells which had conquered the world were three-ply with reinforcing rings. In the mid 1970s Ludwig moved from this configuration to six-ply maple shells, in part to support the new tom mounts with their massive bases. At this stage Ludwig also changed their production methods, leaving behind steam-bending and moving to the use

Bob Henrit c1970 (left) Henrit is pictured playing a Slingerland kit with Argent. Note the 18" and 22" bass drums as well as the toms mounted on a mini-rack with Swiv-O-Matic holders. Argent enjoyed a top-five hit in the United States with 'Hold Your Head Up' in 1972. Since the early 1980s, Henrit has played drums for The Kinks.

Neil Peart (above) Peart was probably the most worshipped rock drummer of the 1980s, and his band Rush has achieved a rare stability. Peart is meticulous with his drumming and his equipment, doing wonders for the sales of Tama, Ludwig and DW. Previously he played Slingerland (above), whose wood snare remained his favourite.

Slingerland Concorde 11N kit (right) This magnificent kit in copper cladding is from Slingerland's 1973 catalogue, a blaze of dazzling flames

and sparkling pearls. Slingerland were in peak form, making great drums with maple shells and reinforcing rings. The Set-O-Matic tom holders had clever all-round positioning; the Super-Speed bass pedals had twin compression springs adjustable from above.

Pink Floyd sleeve (above) The Floyd kit below was used at the time of the band's Dark Side Of The Moon, one of the biggest selling records of all time.

Nick Mason's Ludwig kit 1973 (left) Mason played this kit on Pink Floyd's European stage shows in support of their album Dark Side Of The Moon. The drums were painted by Kate Hepburn, a friend from student days at architectural college. 'The Wave' design is after the painting by Japanese artist Hokusai. Mason was an early convert to double bass drums, and with his unique, expansive, rolling tom tom style was the most visually arresting member of the band. The Floyd generally have preferred to remain in the background while their spectacular stage shows, which they pioneered from the late 1960s, unfurl around them. Sizes here are 14x22, 8x12, 9x13, 14x14 and 16x16.

FOR THE ULTIMATE IN TONAL COMBINATIONS—CONSIDER

OCTA-PLUS OR QUADRA-PLUS......

Ludwig Octa-plus 1973 (above) During the 1970s, as close-miking and multitrack recording became common, single-headed (or 'concert') toms began to catch on in the studio and on stage. Ludwig offered Octa-plus and Quadra-plus 'melodic' toms, so-called because they produced clearly defined pitches.

Billy Cobham (right) Cobham's landmark album Spectrum (1973) combined his mastery of funky grooves with flashes of awesome technique, and confirmed his compositional talent and pioneering use of computers and electronics. In the early 1970s brilliant young jazz drummers brought a new level of technical prowess to power playing. Cobham in particular had an immense influence on the development of rock/jazz drumming and the extended kit. Here he plays his radical transparent acrylic Fibes kit.

of circular moulds. This might all have been necessary, but it cost Ludwig many fans. Were the Americans losing the race?

TAMA, YAMAHA AND PEARL

Take a deep breath, because now everything is going to change dramatically. After the euphoria of the 1960s, the early 1970s brought nothing but misery to the economy of the West, and in particular to Britain. The music revolution which had started in 1963 and gone through to 1973 took a nose-dive when the Middle East oil crisis resulted in quadrupled oil prices. America could no longer afford to buoy up the West as it had done since World War II. The boom period ended abruptly and with dramatic results. Britain was thrown into turmoil with three-day working weeks and nationwide power cuts. Youth reacted to the bleak outlook with the nihilistic racket of punk. In Britain and the rest of the West, including the US, large-scale unemployment, not seen since back in the 1930s, returned. Manufacturing industries and practices seen as outdated were ruthlessly eliminated.

The way was clear for the Japanese to rise from post-war misery to become an outstandingly efficient superpower. The next decade would see the rise of the now familiar Japanese drum companies – Pearl, Tama and Yamaha. West Germany was in a similar position to Japan – with nowhere to go but up. They also prospered. Sonor drums changed from also-rans marketed rather feebly as Chicago Star kits in the mid 1970s, to the spare-no-expense quality of the proudly titled Signature of the 1980s.

One of those major shifts in fortunes which has characterised the 20th century thus exposed the British and American fool's-paradise economies, even as these countries led the world in music and fashion.

The Japanese companies were not new. Yamaha has been around since the end of the 19th century. Hoshino (Tama) was established in 1908, while Pearl got going immediately after World War II. Ivor Arbiter – surprise, surprise – was importing Pearl into Britain "almost before Ludwig", in other words at the end of the 1950s. Pearl actually made their first pro series, called President, in 1966. But it was the early 1970s when the Japanese really got into gear. So far they had mostly been exporting cheap, nondescript kits for others to badge. When the Western currencies took a dive these kits suddenly didn't look

such a bargain. For the Japanese it was a question of what to do. Should they call it a day, or go up-market? Should they risk producing quality instruments they could put their own name to and which they could market at realistic prices? Hoshino, at the time producing pretty forgettable Star kits, thought that this was the way forward, and in 1974 they introduced the brandname Tama. By the late 1970s Tama, Yamaha and Pearl were all producing professional-quality kits.

The Japanese knew that to succeed they had to leap-frog the Americans in quality, innovation and price. The rock scene in the 1970s was scaling up prodigiously – a whole new level of drum kit dependability and flexibility was demanded. This would require large-scale investment, intensive research and development (R&D), and expensive re-tooling. The Japanese companies faced the task head on. Looking at the drum kit with fresh eyes, they were able to spot design flaws, particularly in hardware, which drummers had got used to and manufacturers didn't think it necessary to change or improve. And the Japanese drum companies sensibly sought out the advice and co-operation of major artists.

Tama turned to Billy Cobham, who in the early 1970s was arguably the world's most technically innovative drummer. Although Cobham came up through jazz, he, like Buddy Rich before him, made an incalculable impression on rock drumming and drummers. By the time he hit the headlines he'd devoted half his life to developing a more flexible approach, leading with left or right hand, varying his stick grip, and moving his feet up and down the pedals to different 'stations'. This gave him a more centred, ambidextrous approach. Inevitably he had loads of ideas for expanding the ordinary drum kit.

In the early 1970s Cobham had his gear personally customised by Al Duffy of the Professional Drum Center in New York. However, joining Tama meant Cobham's ideas could be tested on a much larger scale, some of them reaching the marketplace. Cobham's gong drum duly took its place in Tama's catalogue. But the first thing Tama did was to introduce the boom cymbal stand in 1974 as part of the Titan hardware line with wide double-braced tripod bases. Boom stands had become necessary in order to reach cymbals over rows of concert toms. From 1975 Tama R&D was run by Naohiro Yasuda. As a design engineer from outside the drum world he brought new solutions to old problems. One for which drummers will always be thankful was the introduction of nylon restriction-bushings in the joints of stands. This solved the problem of stripped threads which had plagued drummers for years. No longer would heavy-handed roadies get that soundcheck itch to abuse the drummer's stands with a pair of pliers. Next came the 'multi-clamp' which allowed drummers to add on extra appendages to existing cymbal stands. Both these innovations in drum hardware have since become standard throughout the industry.

THE AMERICANS SLIP AWAY

By now the Americans were looking nervously over their shoulders. It's not that they were making poor drums – although some weren't as good as they had been in earlier decades. But there were labour problems and increasing raw material costs. Still they put up a fight and kept delivering new products right through to the end of the 1970s when the Japanese really started to pull away.

For example, the mid 1970s saw the introduction of the Rogers MemriLoc hardware system. This was altogether more bulky than the Swiv-O-Matic, employing 1″ diameter matt silver tubing. But the *pièce de résistance* was the MemriLoc concept itself, a simple drum-key-tightened ring clamp which prevented slippage and reproduced exactly the same set-up heights and angles every time. Memory locks have also since become standard fittings.

Ludwig had met the heavy era with their Atlas line of hardware which graduated to the Hercules line in 1978 with tubular construction like the Rogers MemriLoc. And Slingerland followed the old Swiv-O-Matic by introducing their Set-O-Matic hardware in the early 1970's. Boom cymbal stands had been introduced by all the major manufacturers, and they reached something of a peak in the early 1980s with the crane-like Grandstand, part of Slingerland's Magnum Force line.

In the end, however, all this activity was piecemeal and no doubt covered up a lot of desperation behind the scenes. As the 1980s arrived both the Rogers and Slingerland names descended into a travesty of their former selves, appearing sporadically on insipid products made in Asia over which I think we'll draw a veil and keep a dignified silence. However,

the good news is that Slingerland has regained some credibility in the mid 1990s with Gregg Bissonette (David Lee Roth band) endorsing their drums.

BACK IN THE EAST

Tama, Pearl and Yamaha each in turn made an enormous impact. But it was Tama who made the biggest initial impression with Billy Cobham, the definitive jazz rock fusionist. Cobham was followed to Tama by Stewart Copeland, the definitive rock-reggae fusionist, and Bill Bruford, the intelligent voice of progressive rock. In 1983 Tama also secured the approval of Rush's Neil Peart, the rock world's biggest pollwinner of the 1980s.

Cobham helped design Tama's Superstar line, with classic six-ply birch shells. Copeland, a revelation with the Police, sold a lot of Imperial Stars for Tama, with heavyweight nine-ply shells, reinforcing rings and an interior anti-moisture lining of Zola-Coat. With the introduction of the slightly thinner shelled Artstar, a six-ply sandwich of birch with outer plies of South American cordia which Neil Peart had requested, Tama was just about top dog.

EXPORTING A LOUD SOUND

Pearl started in 1946 making music stands which were then converted to cymbal stands. The first kits, according to Roy Holliday, Pearl's British manager during the 1980s, were inevitably copies of American drums. Holliday says, "The first 20″ Pearl drum I ever saw had seven tension lugs! But it didn't take them long to get it right and the first full kit looked like a Slingerland." Pearl's bass pedals and tom brackets of the 1970s were also strongly influenced by Rogers' Swiv-O-Matic.

Pearl had been the first Japanese name to penetrate the UK and the US, turning heads with top jazz stars such as Art Blakey, Louie Bellson and the *Tonight Show*'s Ed Shaughnessy. In Britain Pearl started to make serious progress when in February 1979 Gerry Evans and Glyn Thomas set up Pearl UK in north London, a stone's throw from the pre-war Premier factory. Evans and Thomas moved on, and Roy Holliday became manager in September 1980.

During Holliday's tenure Pearl launched the Export budget drum kit which was to become the world's biggest seller. "They wanted to call it Loud Sound," Holliday says, "but I suggested

Billy Cobham 1980 (above)
Cobham was Tama's most prized
endorser in the early 1980s. Although
he came up through jazz, he made a
big impression on rock drumming and
drummers. Cobham had considerable
influence on the design of Tama's
Superstar kit, with its six-ply birch
straight-sided shells. He also introduced
the mounted gong bass drum, since
adopted by Bruford and Phillips (right).

Camco pedal (below) This bass pedal
is based on a classic design which has
seen success in various forms. Gretsch
put their name on it, for example, and
called it the Gretsch Floating Action
pedal. When Camco was dissolved,
Tama took over the hardware side and
marketed this pedal, which is
suitably stamped Camco
By Tama.

Stewart Copeland (above) During
the late 1970s the Police with
drummer Copeland were the world's
top group. The trio explored a dynamic
range rare in rock by abruptly jumping
from raucous, speedy punk into the
half-time groove of reggae. Copeland
used a blue Tama Imperial Star kit with
the heads cranked up to extreme
hardness for his distinctive attack.

Bill Bruford 1982 (left) Bruford started out with Yes (1971 sleeve, inset) and is the most exploratory of the influential British drummers who emerged in the late 1960s. A typically idiosyncratic Bruford set-up (left) includes Tama snare and bass drums, Octoban-style Dragon drums, gong drum, 14" Roto-tom, and Simmons electronic pads. Bruford has also worked with King Crimson and Al DiMeola, as well as on his own solo projects.

Simon Phillips (right) Phillips is the acknowledged super-talent of British rock fusion drumming. As a sessionman he's played with Britain's great rock guitarist Jeff Beck (1980 sleeve, inset), and as a talented writer, engineer and producer fronted his own band Protocol. Phillips was part of the design team for the Tama Starclassic kit (right) which incorporates the classic elements of die-cast rims with ultra-thin nine-ply straight-sided shells.

JEFF BECK

Tama Mastercraft snare drums c1982 (left) Tama was the first of the Japanese companies to offer a comprehensive range of snare drums in a wide variety of woods and metals.

Royal Star 5x14 snare drum 1972 (right) Before introducing their Tama brandname in 1974, the Hoshino company of Japan marketed Star drums. This heavily chromed snare, with Dyna-Sonic style parallel action, was used extensively by sessionman Charlie Morgan — and was known to producers as the 'DTS' (the Deadly Teenage Snare). During the early 1980s Tama developed an impressive range of Mastercraft snare drums (above) in bell brass, rosewood, fibreglass, birch, cordia/birch mix, and steel. They had die-cast rims, roller-action snare strainer and choice of steel, bell brass and aircraft wire snares.

Export. I explained to them that after the war in the UK we made things of special quality 'for export only', which became a byword for quality." The timing of the Export was lucky. Yamaha and Tama weren't concentrating on cheap kits, and Premier were in financial trouble in the mid 1980s (and were eventually bought by Yamaha in 1987).

The Export brought real no-nonsense design and quality of construction to the budget market. It had everything you needed, was pretty bland and totally reliable – a familiar 1980s Japanese success story. Over the succeeding years the Export has been continually improved while the price has if anything dropped. The original basic Pearl Export design is the blueprint for countless Taiwanese clone kits which are sold in every country throughout the world.

Like the other Japanese companies, Pearl worked hard to establish an identity during the 1980s with new products, some of which were more successful than others. The Free Floating System of 1983 was an interesting concept which had limited success. The FFS snare drum had interchangeable shells of different materials – copper, brass, steel or maple. The shell 'floated' inside the frame made by the top and bottom die-cast rims joined together by tubular pipe lugs. The lugs were not attached to the shell, so the shell was allowed to resonate unimpeded. This foreshadowed to an extent the obsession with 'resonance isolation' which would overtake the drum world over the next decade.

While Yamaha and Tama concentrated more on the pro end of the market, Pearl was successful at all levels, growing into the biggest drum company in the world, with a huge plant in Taichung, Taiwan. Pearl offered a wider range than anybody else, including several lines of pro kits in both birch and maple plus various budget and starter kits. Pearl endorsers have included the top players in every style of music, names like Jeff Porcaro, Phil Collins, Ian Paice of Deep Purple, Tico Torres of Bon Jovi, Tommy Lee of Mötley Crüe, and the formidable jazz and funk master Dennis Chambers.

THE LOOK OF THE EIGHTIES

At the end of 1969 in *Down Beat* magazine the session drummer John Guerin was shown endorsing a Yamaha drum kit which looks remarkably like a Ringo-style Ludwig in oyster pearl. But by 1976 Yamaha's designer Takashi Hagiwara

('Hagi') had produced a masterstroke with a studio-friendly kit which was to become closely associated with the greatest of all studio drummers, Steve Gadd (who is probably best known for work such as Steely Dan's 'Aja' and Paul Simon's 'Fifty Ways To Leave Your Lover').

The Yamaha 9000 Recording Custom is the most successful pro kit since the Ludwig Super Classic. The 9000 recently celebrated its twentieth anniversary and is only just now showing signs of being out of step with fashion. Considering the enormous changes during this period it's an amazing achievement for Hagiwara that the kit was so nearly perfect from the beginning. As the RC9000 increased in popularity through the early 1980s it forced the pace of all the other drum manufacturers, particularly Tama and Pearl. The adoption of lacquered finishes and previously unfashionable flush, hi-tension bracing, which replaced Yamaha's earlier bullet style lugs, became *the* look of the 1980s.

Flush bracing means that the lug stretches the whole depth of the shell instead of having separate short lugs at either end. Theoretically this takes some of the stress away from the shell itself. Premier drums had long been famous for their superbly chromed flush-braced lugs, but this image had become out of line with everyone else. They finally changed to single lugs – just as Yamaha's kit appeared with a design almost identical to Premier's classic. Ironically, after Premier changed to single lugs they found themselves going in the opposite direction to all the others, who were busy copying the Yamaha model.

The 9000 introduced new standards in lacquered external finishes, drawing on Yamaha's many years of experience in making pianos. The interior was also piano-like, rather than the usual hard lacquered or painted finish, and this contributed to the dark, warm sound. The shell had a Gretsch-like six-ply straight-sided configuration, though of birch not maple. And the shells were perfectly round as a result of the special Air-Seal shell making system. Along with Tama's Superstar, Yamaha's 9000 kit set the fashion for birch shells over the next decade.

The Yamaha kit also had great hardware, at once graceful, superbly engineered and supremely functional. Never had a tom bracket been so easy to position and so steadfast. And yet if you look closely it still embodies the two major principles of Rogers' Swiv-O-Matic: the hexagonal rod, and the ball clamp.

60

FLOOR STANDS AND REMOTE HI-HATS

The Ludwig Octaplus introduced the idea of floor stands right at the beginning of the 1970s. These were similar to timbale type stands, suspending rows of concert toms over the kit. But Steve Gadd made stands for lower floor toms hip. He preferred to use 10x14 and 12x15 toms mounted on a dual floor stand, rather than the traditional floor toms with legs. This type of kit set-up became known as a 'fusion' kit during the 1980s. It was taken a step further by Dave Weckl, who came to fame with Chick Corea's Elektric Band and is one of the most talented of the post-Gadd generation. Weckl added another tom to the left of his hi-hat, an idea that stemmed from the teaching of Gary Chester (New York's answer to Hal Blaine) who played on literally hundreds of hit records during the 1960s and 1970s, including 'I'm A Believer' (Monkees), 'Do You Believe In Magic' (Lovin' Spoonful), 'Stand By Me' (Ben E King) and 'Brown Eyed Girl' (Van Morrison).

In order to be flexible, Chester devised a studio set-up where the left side of his kit mirrored the right side. As well as having a floor tom to the left, Chester put a second hi-hat to the right. This 'remote' hi-hat, newly championed by the likes of Weckl, caught on in the 1980s. The remote hi-hat was mounted on the right but operated via a cable joined to a pedal placed to the left of the normal hi-hat. Eventually most players were happy to have the secondary hi-hat permanently closed – which obviated the need for the cable and left-side pedal. The hi-hat could simply be mounted in a convenient space to the right (something previously used in the 1930s) and this became known as the X-hat.

RACK IT UP

When Carl Palmer built his stainless steel kit in 1975 he reverted to the 1930s console-type idea and mounted the drums, cymbals and mikes. This was definitely a one-off, but in 1980 Jeff Porcaro, touring with his band Toto, designed a rack for the modern era with the help of drum technician Paul Jamieson. This was put into production in 1983 as the Pearl DR-1 drum rack. It had a square cross section of lightweight aluminium on which all the hardware for the toms and cymbals could be clamped.

Later rack designs from Tama (Power Tower) and Yamaha (Super Rack) favoured tubular chromed steel. As the 1980s progressed, racks started to surround the drummer, ending in full blown cages. What was that about wild beasts? Now cymbals could be suspended from above, yet another throwback to the 1930s and swan-neck stands. For a decade drummers competed for the biggest set-up. AJ Pero of Twisted Sister had a four-bass drum kit painted as trash cans with a ludicrous forest of cymbal arm extensions – a kids' construction set from hell. But the wildest cage has to be that of Mötley Crüe's Tommy Lee. This was an amazing mechanical riser which lifted off the ground and turned a complete somersault while Tommy was soloing.

OLD SNARE, NEW SNARE

Through the 1980s the Japanese systematically picked over every aspect of the drum kit. But they had trouble with snare drums. Steve Gadd happily endorsed his Yamaha 9000 but wouldn't leave home without his Ludwig Supraphonic 400 snare drum. Andy Newmark, another Yamaha enthusiast, put it this way: "The Ludwig became the workhorse of the industry. All you ever saw in the studio was the 400 – nine out of ten drummers had one. It was bright, quick, dark and flexible. Jazz guys, rock guys and symphony guys could all use it. It's not that the Japanese snare drums were bad, just that Ludwig hit on a magic drum."

Jeff Porcaro and the French drummer Manu Katché (who found fame with Peter Gabriel) were other devotees. Porcaro regularly used a Ludwig in the studio, although live he preferred a vintage Radio King with a deep shell and the inside re-veneered to produce a hard reflective surface. He reckoned this was as live as a metal drum, but more musical.

Drum companies have learned to turn a blind eye to their endorsers' penchant for different snare drums. Buddy Rich often played a Fibes; Neil Peart had a favourite Slingerland for years; Chad Smith (Red Hot Chili Peppers) today may use an Australian Brady or a vintage Ludwig; and Keith Moon was partial to Gretsch wood snare drums. Moon's roadie Bill Harrison told me that Keith had at least three.

Harrison also told me about Moon, short of money during a bout of drinking, popping from The Ship pub in Wardour Street, central London, next door to Henrit's Drumstore and exchanging a Gretsch snare for some ready cash. Harrison would of course have to return the next day and retrieve the

61

Tommy Aldridge Carbon Custom kit (right) This unique kit with twin 24" bass drums was made for Tommy Aldridge, the HM master of Black Oak Arkansas, Whitesnake, and Manic Eden. Carbon fibre is an "ultra-rigid space age composite", say Yamaha, and Aldridge claimed the kit has "more top-end and more low-end than any other drums".

Mike Bordin (above) Bordin of Faith No More has shown that Yamaha's RC9000 kit is not just for jazz-fusion. He's a remarkable drummer who plays open-handed on a conventional 'right-handed' kit, positioning his oversize toms horizontally, yet managing to attack them ferociously with bravery and Olympic stamina. Beneath the wild image there is a dedicated musical mind feeding on influences from Tony Williams to British post-punk drummers like Killing Joke's Paul Ferguson.

62

Yamaha Recording Custom kit (with YESS) 1995 (right) The RC9000 set the pace in the 1980s with birch shells finished with piano lacquer, flush-braced lugs and floor-mounted tom tom stands. This was the look adopted by the major drum companies up to the late 1980s when 'retro' heralded the return of tubular lugs and maple shells. The RC9000 celebrated its 20th birthday in 1995, relaunched with YESS tom mounts (the Yamaha Enhanced Sustain System, right). Developed in 1993, the System was fitted to the Maple Custom line, first seen in 1991, which introduced new low-mass button lugs, 'nodally mounted' by a single bolt Noble & Cooley-style.
Sizes here are 16x22, 8x8, 9x10, 10x12, 13x15 and 14x16, plus 6½x14 snare.

Steve Gadd (right) Throughout the 1980s Gadd was considered the world's most accomplished drummer, playing everything from the simplest beat to the preposterously difficult with the same authority, intensity of feeling and taste. Steely Dan's *Aja* (1977, inset) is a perfect example. Gadd defined the 1980s drum sound, using twin-ply heads on the Yamaha RC9000 for a deep, warm, resonant tone. He showed how to get a singing tone from a small 10" tom and amazing depth from a floor-mounted 10x14 tom, leading to the concept of the 'fusion kit'. Gadd invariably used a standard Ludwig Supraphonic 400 snare.

63

Andy Newmark 1983 (right) Newmark once told this author that he "lives on the planet of the eighth-note". Certainly he plays the backbeat with more conviction than just about anybody, driving artists as diverse as Sly & The Family Stone, Carly Simon, James Taylor and Roxy Music (right). Newmark prefers a simple kit with a 24" bass drum and crash cymbals up impossibly high (after Dino Danelli). He's not one for a lot of fills, but when he goes for that small 12" tom it had better be tightened on its stand.

Cozy Powell (below) Powell grew up sparring with John Bonham for the best gigs in Birmingham, England. In 1974 he achieved a rare drum-solo hit record, 'Dance With The Devil'. His vast experience includes stints with Black Sabbath, Rainbow, and Whitesnake.

drum. Today, of course, most pro drummers have a collection of different snare drums for different situations, and the endorsed drum companies understand that they may be different makes. When recording, a producer may request a certain drum or even bring one himself for the drummer to play. Top session players have dozens. Dave Mattacks, for instance, one of Britain's most consistently popular session drummers (he's worked with everyone from Paul McCartney to Jethro Tull, from Sandy Denny to Brian Eno), has a quite fabulous collection of snare drums of every conceivable make and vintage, and I can personally attest that they're all tuned up and ready to go.

POWER SIZES

Yet another consequence of the increasing din of rock had come along by the 1980s when drum shell sizes started mysteriously to gain a few inches to reach so-called 'power' depths, where for example 8x12 became 10x12. Tama in 1982 offered Superstar drums with the new X-tra depth (for example 16x22) as an alternative to the standard depth (for example 14x22). The following year the new Artstar drums were introduced in the X-tra power depths only – in this case an extra 3″ added to each tom tom. Around this time all the manufacturers started to offer 'power' sizes which became standard for the next ten years.

Through the 1980s snare drums also got deeper, going from the standard 5″ up to 8″ and sometimes to 10 or 12 inches. Then, later in the 1980s, the pendulum swung back and shallow 'piccolo' snare drums, with a tighter, higher pitched sound, returned after an absence of 20 or more years, with many catalogues, from Pearl and Tama to Ludwig and Sonor, soon featuring 3x13 drums.

TALKING HEADS

The Japanese shook the industry to its roots – and maybe that was no bad thing. After half a century a fresh approach was needed. But not all was gloom in America. For example the two cymbal companies, Zildjian and its breakaway Sabian, along with the drum head company Remo, all continued to prosper and carve out their own paths.

Remo never let go of the number one position. There was healthy competition from Ludwig and Evans, but not from

Japan. Remo had long produced three weights of head – the lightweight Diplomat, the industry standard Ambassador, and the heavyweight Emperor. But two landmark variations were introduced in the 1970s.

First was the Controlled Sound (CS) Black Dot, which had a reinforcing circle of Mylar stuck to its centre, slightly reducing the overtones. Apparently the dot was added to cut down on the number of bass drum heads that Buddy Rich was stomping through. But the Black Dot head quickly became a favourite of rock drummers, and Ludwig copied it with their Silver Dot Rockers.

Then came the Remo Pinstripe (1977) which was two clear layers of Diplomat-weight Mylar bonded around the outer collar, producing a darker, more damped sound. This was a response to the Evans Hydraulic, the double-thickness head which has a thin film of oil in between, and which was popular at the time. The Pinstripe proved more adaptable than the rather heavy Hydraulic and became virtually standard issue throughout the 1980s. It only started to wane when the return to brighter sounds during the 1990s restored the Ambassador to fashionable popularity.

WHEN IS A HEAD A DRUM?

While the rest of the American drum industry struggled, Remo chose the early 1980s to branch into the drum business. The move stemmed from experiments with heads which had been chemically treated to give them a 'memory'. These heads retained their tension and didn't require tuning. The Remo Pre-Tuned System (PTS) appeared in 1982 and it was a real eye-opener. When you hear it said that most of a drum's sound comes from the head you probably don't take it literally. Well, try to get hold of a Remo pre-tuned head. Hold the edge of the head with your fingers, strike it, and yes... on its own it really does sound like a drum. Pretty freaky.

Remo produced rather feeble PTS kits for the heads to clip onto. They weren't overly successful. But a couple of years later, in 1985, Remo moved into the proper drum kit arena with the Encore line. The Encore featured shells made from a material called Acousticon, which is wood fibre impregnated with resin. They were covered in a coloured plastic material called Quadura. Despite the usual misgivings about synthetic shells, Remo successfully won over many great players, including

Ricky Lawson and Terry Bozzio (who came to prominence with Frank Zappa). And the drums have been continually improved: today's professional Mastertouch line is punchy, loud and resonant, although the latest version, called VenWood, bows to drummer's conservatism and has a veneer of real maple bonded to the outside of the Acousticon R shell.

THE CYMBAL SECRET

Like drum heads, cymbals have come a long way since the 1960s. When Ringo got stoked up he played his ride cymbal on the edge, turning the sound into a swirling wash of white noise, creating an excitement which is a feature of early Beatles records. The reason this happened was that cymbals at this time were generally quite small and lightweight. Another trick was to put rivets in the cymbal. Bobby Elliott recorded The Hollies' classic hits on a riveted 18″ Paiste Formula 602.

However, as bands got louder cymbals got broken. Whereas the earlier jazz drummers had wanted larger cymbal diameters for deeper sounds, the rockers wanted brighter sounds from heavier cymbals that wouldn't break. In Europe the Swiss company Paiste decided early on to make cymbals tailored to the needs of rock drummers. The Giant Beat cymbals of the mid 1960s gave way in 1971 to the 2002 series which had a clean sound able to cut through increasingly loud amplification. Paiste was well placed to win over many of the British-based rock pioneers like John Bonham, Carl Palmer, Jon Hiseman (John Mayall, Colosseum), Bill Bruford and Stewart Copeland.

Paiste was distributed in the US by Ludwig who included budget Paistes with their kits and stamped them Ludwig Standard. From the mid 1960s Ludwig imported the top grade Paiste Formula 602. Paiste soon attracted name American players including session masters Jim Keltner (John Lennon, Ry Cooder etc) and Jeff Porcaro.

As Paiste cymbals became increasingly popular, Zildjian played up their centuries-old heritage, emphasising the mystique of ancient craftsmanship and 'secret' processes. Paiste meanwhile replied with talk of efficient, consistent, up-to-the-minute metallurgy, as did German company Meinl a little later. Over the years this transatlantic squabble has sometimes sunk to a petty level, and has proved to be both irritating and confusing for the average drummer looking on.

The actual substance of the 'cymbal wars' concerned both the alloys used in cymbal making and the casting processes involved. Cymbals are made from copper mixed with varying amounts of tin, nickel or zinc. The traditional cymbal alloy is bronze (copper plus tin). Top line cymbals are 80 per cent copper to 20 per cent tin ('B20'), and this is the bronze used for expensive Zildjians, Sabians, (Italian) Ufips and (Turkish) Istanbuls, among others. Paiste spent from 1980 to 1989 developing its own Signature Line bronze alloy, the formulation of which it has kept secret – as if to say we too can play the game of 'secret processes'.

However, what set Paiste apart in the early rock days was their use from 1963 of another bronze alloy, known as B8, that contains eight per cent tin with 92 per cent copper. This was specially developed for the Giant Beat and 2002 lines. It rankled with the Americans for a while, but eventually they responded in the best way – by making their own B8 cymbals, today's Zildjian Scimitars and Edges, and Sabian B8s.

The processes involved in turning bronze alloys into shimmering cymbals include casting, rolling, beating, tempering, hammering and lathing. The ancient cymbalsmith's craft was an arduous, sweaty, dirty and highly skilled process. Each cymbal was made by hand, which was definitely hit-and-miss as far as quality control was concerned. Today, each company goes about it all in a slightly different way and with a varying degree of human and machine involvement. As you can deduce from the literally hundreds of different types of cymbal on the market, the variations in manufacture are almost infinite. And over the past couple of decades the cymbal companies have learned how to control each process to 'design' sounds almost at will.

PINK FLOYD, BLACK CYMBALS

Stadium rock and heavy metal continued to grow through the 1980s. Playing at this sort of level, the concept of a ride cymbal with subtlety of sustain and overtones is pretty well lost. Drummers were looking for a ride with clear stick definition, the stability of a table-top, and killer volume. Zildjian produced Earth rides, while Paiste launched their Rude series (1980) which were exactly that: cymbals which had forgone the final lathing and finishing processes that gave them their tonal subtlety. By the mid 1980s the variety of cymbal types was

Chris Whitten (right) Whitten graduated from the London session scene to land a dream gig with Paul McCartney during the late 1980s, and then moved on to play with Dire Straits in the early 1990s. He was probably the first British drummer to obtain a full set of Noble & Cooley Star drums in 1989. These fine drums take 16 weeks to hand-craft, and feature solid-shell maple tom toms in unusual 'half ratio' sizes: 6x12, 7x14, and 8x16.

Noble & Cooley kit (right) In 1854 Silas Noble and James P Cooley started making rope-tensioned drums (see inset picture). However, it was not until the early 1980s that they entered the modern drumming world. The mid-1990s CD Maples kit (right) has six- and eight-ply shells in a choice of depths for each diameter, and die-cast or flanged rims. Air-vent holes are hidden beneath the arches of the low mass lugs which are springless and hum-free solid castings. The RIMS mounts have also been adapted to suspend the shells from below the lugs, increasing sustain and easing the changing of heads. N&C drums are finished in environmentally safe paint.

Noble & Cooley Custom Design CD-Maples Kit 1995 (below) Note the powder-coated hardware.

Phil Collins (above) Collins is one of many top players who appreciate Noble & Cooley's Classic SS (solid shell) snare drums. From 1984 these drums spearheaded the 'retro' vintage movement. They feature solid maple steam-bent ¼" shells, with 'nodally mounted' low-mass tubular brass lugs, cast rims and strainers.

Remo Liberator 8x14 ProKit snare drum c1988 (below) This drum is finished in chrome Quadura covering over an Acousticon SE shell. It has quick-change Powersnap lugs, as well as low, medium and high PTS pre-tuned heads, and Remo's 3-State Muff'l sound control system.

67

Carl Palmer c1987 (above) Remo Belli and Carl Palmer share an abiding interest in unusual shell materials. The mid-1980s Encore had shells made from a compressed fibre material called Acousticon. The Encore also featured Dynamax hardware and Powersnap lugs (replaced with stylish cutaway lugs in Remo's MasterTouch series of 1988).

Ricky Lawson 1992 (left) Lawson is one of today's most in-demand drummers, powering the stadium shows of Michael Jackson, Phil Collins and Steely Dan. His mile-deep groove is exemplified on Anita Baker's acclaimed 1986 album Rapture (inset above) and Whitney Houston's mega-hit 'I Will Always Love You'. Lawson is pictured (left) with his Michael Jackson Dangerous tour kit: Remo MasterTouch drums with RIMS mounts and Paiste Signature cymbals. MasterTouch drums have Acousticon 'R' 516 (⁵⁄₁₆") shells, now available as VenWood with an outer veneer of real maple.

Terry Bozzio (above) Bozzio made an early mark with Frank Zappa, and led the way during the mid 1990s with his solo concerts for extended drum kit.

really broadening out. Zildjian came up with the radically modern looking Z series, which are unlathed but polished to a gleaming Brilliant finish and which feature computerised hammering patterns. Paiste did the unthinkable and introduced coloured cymbals, the Color Sound 5 series which came in black, red, blue or green. Nick Mason of Pink Floyd had asked for black cymbals for *The Wall* tour and Paiste got to work. Applying colour was easy... but then they had to make them sound good.

After the death of Avedis Zildjian III in 1979 the heirs to the throne, Armand and Robert Zildjian, couldn't reconcile their differences and they split. Robert took over the Zildjian plant in Meductic, Canada, and formed the Sabian cymbal company. Sabian got going in the early 1980s and has been a real success story, providing excellent competition for Zildjian and Paiste. Their top notch cymbals, HH (Hand Hammered) and AA ('and 'ammered?), established Sabian's reputation, and they soon branched out with as many varieties as Zildjian and Paiste. Equally impressive is their list of endorsers, from Rod Morgenstein and Phil Collins to the newer-generation Stephen Perkins of Porno For Pyros and Sean Kinney of Alice in Chains.

REVISITING THE HERITAGE

Americans are often envious of other nations' long histories. But when it comes to the drum kit the Americans have it. Throughout the Japanese revolution discerning drummers sought out vintage snare drums that supplied a tone which modern drums simply did not have. We're back in Radio King territory again, along with Gretsch Gladstones or Leedy Broadways as well as brass-shell drums like Ludwig Black Beautys and Leedy Black Elites.

The Achilles heel of the Japanese makers was their snare drums. Enter Noble & Cooley, who'd been making toy drums in Massachusetts since the mid 19th century. A local musician, on finding that Noble & Cooley did steam-bending of shells, asked them if they could help restore an old Radio King. A light went on at Nobel & Cooley and they started to think about making a solid shell professional drum themselves. It took them another six years to get round to it, but in 1984 the impressive result was the Noble & Cooley Solid Shell (SS) maple snare drum with solid, low-mass, brass-tubular lugs and die cast rims. It was a modern realisation of old principles and it became an icon for

the whole classic and retro movement which is still going strong today. The Japanese competitiveness had gradually forced up the quality of straight sided, medium-thickness ply shells. Thin shells with reinforcing hoops looked very old fashioned. But once the retro movement started whole kits would be built with thin shells and reinforcing hoops again, and – most surprisingly – with tube lugs. What's more, they would be made from traditional American/Canadian maple rather than birch.

The Americans could now see a small window of opportunity. It was obvious that competing on a large scale with the Japanese was no longer possible, but smaller, custom-building companies started to emerge. Over the next decade traditional-style maple snare drums would be made by the likes of Joe Montineri, Solid, Pork Pie, Legend, Trick, Drum Factory, Ayotte, and Bison. Noble & Cooley expanded their operation in the late 1980s by introducing onto the market their new Star line of complete kits with solid shells.

ONE NEW NAME, THREE OLD ONES

One of the companies which emerged in the 1980s has grown into a market leader in America. This is Drum Workshop (DW) which is directly descended from that grand figure of American drums, George Way. DW started out with hardware, bought the tools and dies from the doomed Camco company in 1979, and when they eventually went into making drums were able finally to make a success of the turret lug design made famous by George Way and Camco.

DW founders Don Lombardi and John Good are committed to producing maple drums with no compromises on quality. All of the DW kits are custom selected and John Good personally 'timbre-matches' the shells prior to assembly and tuning. Before leaving the factory, each shell is marked with its fundamental resonant pitch.

Ludwig, Gretsch and Slingerland were the three great names of American drums which – just about – survived the Japanese revolution. Ludwig were helped out of the doldrums by Neil Peart's late-1980s decision to test out a selection of kits in *Modern Drummer* magazine. To his surprise at the time he found Ludwig was the nearest to the sound he was looking for. Since Peart was probably the most worshipped rock drummer of the decade, many young drummers suddenly saw Ludwig in

68

Chester Thompson (left) Thompson played with Weather Report and Frank Zappa before his long association with Genesis and Phil Collins. Sonor's flagship Signature line of 1980 was updated to the Special Edition Signature in 1991 with HiLite-style lug insulation. Thompson's bubinga Signature kit shown here has paired 18x22 bass drums and a cast bronze snare. For recording Thompson prefers a smaller HiLite or a Designer heavy maple kit.

Sonor catalogue (above) Developed by the Link family from 1875, the German Sonor company relinquished the reins to Hohner in 1991.

Sonor Designer kit (left) This is the latest line from Sonor and, in keeping with the company's reputation for extravagance, is probably the most luxurious offered by any major manufacturer today. It follows the 1990s trend for drummers to 'design' their own kits from multiple options. Shells are chosen from birch or two thicknesses of maple ('lite' or heavy'); shell depth is offered in standard (8x12), power (10x12) or square (12x12) sizes; and there's even a choice of lug type — single-ended or full length. Finishes include solid colour lacquers, sparkle lacquers and stains. The Sonor logo of two mallets is incorporated in many aspects of the design, such as the lugs and the enormous bass drum spurs. This kit has single lugs and standard tom sizes, and features Sonor's 'Total Acoustic Resonance' mounting system. Note also the unusual bass drum knob tensioners.

Will Calhoun (above) Calhoun drove the powerhouse rock-funk quartet Living Colour. Their 1993 album Stain (inset left) includes a fine live version of the band's sleazy-funky hit 'Love Rears Its Ugly Head'. In the shot above Calhoun has added an extra small bass drum to his solid yellow lacquer Designer Kit.

GENISTA

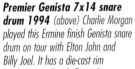

Premier catalogue 1994 (left)
Following the success of the company's Signia line, Premier launched Genista drums in 1994. They have seven-ply birch shells, Premier's traditional wood of choice, but, unusually for Premier, have no reinforcing rings.

Elton John sleeve (right) *Charlie Morgan first toured with Elton John in the fall of 1985, and has recorded several albums — including Made In England (1995, right) — using Premier drums and Paiste cymbals. Morgan is one of London's busiest rock session players and has worked with Paul McCartney, Tina Turner, Gary Moore, Kate Bush, Go West, Alison Moyet, Linda Thompson, and Wham.*

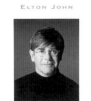

ELTON JOHN

Made in England

Charlie Morgan's Premier Signia kit 1992 (front, right) *Morgan's maple-shell Signia was customised in black and white for Elton John's recent world tour, stage-designed by Versace. The low-tech rack was made from Kee-Klamp by Morgan and tech Pete Mills.*

Premier snare drums (t...
From Charlie Morgan's kit, th... Signia (left) has a maple sh... reinforcing rings and chrome... rims, while the 4x14 has a ... and brass-plated rims. Both ... 610 quick-release snare me...

Premier Genista 7x14 snare drum 1994 (above) *Charlie Morgan played this Ermine finish Genista snare drum on tour with Elton John and Billy Joel. It has a die-cast rim on the top and triple-flanged steel on the bottom. Note the internal microphone and external socket.*

Richie Hayward c1975 (below)
Hayward played this black Premier Resonator kit with Little Feat, who blended rock, blues and country with the rolling pulse of New Orleans rhythms. Hayward's unique bustling style, mixing ghost notes and small cymbal splashes, appears pushy — but close your eyes and there's a laidback, half-time groove. Other US drummers endorsing Premier have included Harvey Mason and Rod Morgenstein.

Charlie Morgan's Premier Signia kit 1992 (above; see also front, top right) *Morgan's kit has an 18x22 bass drum, plus 10", 12", 14" and 16" mounted power toms, 4x14 piccolo and 7x14 plain black Signia snare. The hardware is brass-plated; cymbals are special black Paiste Custom Signatures.*

Cindy Blackman (left)
Blackman had this Sonor kit specially built for touring with Lenny Kravitz. It has beech shells with Signature series fittings, and a special White Sparkle lacquer finish. She's avoided Sonor's modern Resonance mounting hardware, opting for traditional floor toms and with the small tom mounted on a snare drum stand. Blackman is the child of a talented musical family and started drumming at the age of eight. Although best known for her rock performances with Kravitz, she has a solid grounding in jazz and has played with pianist Don Pullen and tenor saxophonist Joe Henderson. Her several solo albums include 1992's jazz-flavoured Code Red (inset above) which she dedicated to the great Jazz Messengers drummer Art Blakey.

Nicko McBrain (below) With Iron Maiden, McBrain epitomises the heavy metal drummer — even if his first influence was jazzman Joe Morello. Here, McBrain plays a Sonor Signature.

3

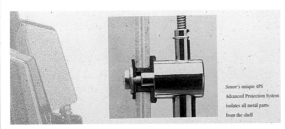

Advanced Projection System (above) Sonor's APS isolates all metal parts from the wooden shell, allowing free shell vibration. While most lugs today are mounted on nylon isolating plinths, the fixing bolts on Sonor's lugs pass through small rubber inserts, so there is no metal-to-wood contact.

Designer hardware (above) In 1996 the Sonor Designer series was awarded the German Federal Design Award, alongside awards for Audi and Porsche. The Total Acoustic Resonance System for mounting the toms is a complete revamp for the 1990s, and as always goes one step further than the opposition. Sonor utilises the familiar ball-and-clamp design, but cleverly achieves extra lateral adjustment by splitting the ball into four segments through which the square steel tom supporting arm passes. The tom is cradled by double RIMS-type brackets with the Acoustigate tensioner, which when tightened or loosened further influences the drum's sustain.

a new light. Gretsch weathered the 1980s with the philosophy 'if it ain't broke then leave it alone'. In truth there wasn't much they could do. They introduced power sizes, and made stabs at modernising hardware, but Gretsch drums have remained pretty well unchanged for years.

So many great drummers are known to have used Gretsch in the studio whatever their current endorsement ads may have shown. It's impossible to put your finger on exactly why, but Gretsch – particularly the company's treasured 'round badge' drums from the 1950s – occupy a special status, in much the same way as do the Slingerland Radio Kings and the Ludwig Supraphonics. Gretsch has the most mystique and it crosses all borders of music: Lars Ulrich (Metallica) has admitted playing Gretsch on occasions in the studio, as did Jeff Porcaro; and recently Vinnie Colaiuta (Sting) has come clean and publicly gone over to endorsing Gretsch.

Finally Slingerland, whose glory days seemed well past, were bought by Gibson in 1995. The next thing we see is Gregg Bissonette – one of rock's true all-rounders, who's played with the Maynard Ferguson big band and as a child idolised Gene Krupa – with a very up-to-the-minute Slingerland kit. The inevitable question looms: are we soon to witness the rejuvenation of both Gretsch and Slingerland?

WHO'S ENDORSING WHO?

Endorsement today is very much tied up with tour support. Rock is big business and touring is ruinously expensive. What drummers generally need is equipment that is reliable and looks good, and they need back-up. They need gear to be available at short notice when they have to fly from one country to another. Most drummers could happily play any top-line drums on stage. But when it comes to the studio, as we have seen with snares, drummers must use whatever is necessary to get exactly the right sound for the track. A good road kit may not be such a good recording kit, and vice versa. These days there are companies who specialise in supplying studio-ready drum kits and snare drums which are known to record well. Many of these drums are vintage instruments.

Another aspect of the endorsement scene is educational or 'clinic' tours. For certain artists these represent a substantial part of their income. Billy Cobham told me in 1991 that one reason for him leaving Tama for the new oriental company

Mapex was that Mapex promised to get him clinic work in Japan, which was very important to his career.

Nonetheless it's confusing when big stars change companies – and many do so frequently. Take Neil Peart again. He's a thoughtful and reliable character, and yet even Peart has gone from Slingerland to Tama to Ludwig to DW. It seems he's always searching and experimenting, and if that means changing allegiances so be it. With all this in mind, it's as well to take endorsement claims with a pinch of salt. Having said that, lasting endorsement relationships do exist – Charlie Watts, for example, has played Gretsch since 1968, and his old mate Ginger Baker has been with Ludwig since 1966.

UNIMPEDED RESONANCE

A major aspect of the Noble & Cooley philosophy was the idea of maximum resonance. Each tube lug is 'nodally' mounted, in other words at the point of least interference with shell vibration. This thinking extended to the idea that all drums should be free to resonate and that conventional mounting hardware was the cause of excessive damping.

Actually, a less restricting way of suspending drums had already been developed. PureCussion RIMS was invented by Gary Gauger and introduced in 1979. RIMS does away with the need to drill and penetrate shells, or to install huge dampening tom mounts on bass drums. The RIMS mount is a semi-circle of steel which attaches to the lugs of the drum by way of four or five rubber grommets. The grommets ensure that there's no metal-to-metal contact, and the whole RIMS mount is bracketed to a floor stand or cymbal stand.

The RIMS concept has taken on enormous significance over the past decade as the idea caught on that a drum should be allowed to resonate totally unimpeded. This is a complete reversal of the 1970s 'cardboard box' sound, but has become so accepted that all the major drum manufacturers had to devise their own resonance-enhancing mounting systems by the 1990s. This coincided with the return to maple, a wood that gives an open, bright sound. All the companies' marketing brains excelled themselves when thinking up names for maple kits with retro classic features and their own versions of isolation mounting: Yamaha had Maple Customs with YESS (Yamaha Enhanced Sustain System). Pearl opted for Masters with ISS (Integrated Suspension System), and Tama offered

Starclassics with Star-Cast Mounting System (licensed from PureCussion). One might also mention Sonor's Total Acoustic Resonance System and Premier's Signia, as well as the most recent of the major oriental companies, Mapex, with their ITS (Isolated Tom System).

Whether this will lead to final curtains for the traditional tom tom bracket remains to be seen. But a word of warning. As Elton John's drummer Charlie Morgan pointed out when Premier were devising their Signia maples, the sound of the drum kit is the sound of an integrated instrument. The drums interact and improve one another's sound, and so maybe the toms *should* be mounted to the bass drum. Just a thought.

WHICH WOOD WORKS WELL?

Throughout much of rock history, the type of wood used in manufacturing drums was not questioned. Drummers were happy to get what they got. And to some extent the manufacturers were too. In the 1950s and 1960s drum companies would generally make only one type of shell. The only way the drummer would get something different would be in the way of sizes – smaller or larger, fewer or more toms, and so on. This also applied to finishes, particularly in the 1970s when rock stars sported purple loon pants and dazzling caftans, leading to a great choice of psychedelic pearls, glitters, moirés, silks and satin swirls.

Back then a drum was made from an indeterminate wood covered with plastic, while the inside was coated with paint – that way you couldn't spot the blemishes. All manner of interior coatings were used, on both good and bad shells. Ludwig, Camco and Hayman had white paint, Gretsch had silver, Rogers had grey fleck, and then later on Pearl had fibreglass and Tama had Zola-Coat. One might well ask: "Once there's a thick coating on the interior, does the type of wood make a jot of difference to the sound?"

Whatever the answer, the situation changed in a big way when natural-lacquered wood finishes – inside and out – took over in the 1980s. We soon moved from a period when most drummers hadn't the foggiest idea what woods were used to make their drums, to a situation where drummers were obsessed with the species of wood, the thickness of the shells, the type of mounting, and so on.

Maple has been the favoured species in north America,

while birch was most common in Europe and Japan. This is largely to do with local availability. But there is a noticeable difference in the quality of timbre imparted by maple, which is bright and 'round' and has longer sustain, and birch, which has a slightly darker more 'contained' and 'directed' studio-friendly sound. This contributed to the success of the birch-shelled Yamaha Recording Custom. Significantly, Pearl referred to their birch drums as studio drums. As bright, resonant sounds have returned to fashion, so has maple.

WHO MAKES THE SHELLS?

Touchy subject this, but the fact is that few drum companies manufacture everything that appears in their brochures, including wooden shells. Why? Well, drum making is a relatively small industry. There are much larger wood-based industries, like furniture making, which call on aeons of woodworking expertise – and where knocking up a few thousand wooden cylinders is a nice little sideline. Particularly since drums are usually made from plywood moulded into the round, there are specialist companies who perhaps do this better than a relatively small drum company could manage. Suffice to say that many American drum shells are and have been manufactured by companies such as Jasper, Keller and Eames. This includes both small and large names: Rogers, Camco, DW, Gretsch and most of the others.

This doesn't mean that all the drums are the same, however, because each drum company gives its supplier specific instructions regarding the number of plies, the thickness, type of wood and so on. And when the drum company gets the bare shells it then sets to work cutting bearing edges and snare beds, as well as carrying out sanding, lacquering and all the other finishing processes.

EVEN BIGGER DRUM KITS

During the 1980s Neil Peart used back-to-back electronic and acoustic kits on a revolving riser. In 1988 Alex van Halen went further with three drum kits – a fibreglass North, a Ludwig acoustic and an electronic – all on a rotating stage. In another demonstration of 1980s restraint Alex managed to play a kit with four bass drums.

Putting on vast shows in huge stadia encourages these mammoth kits. We're talking about larger-than-life kits for

Jonathan Moffett 1995 (right)

Moffett is pictured on the Janet Jackson tour with a DW kit plus Gibraltar rack and Zildjian cymbals. Independent hardware company Gibraltar led the late-1980s market for competitive racks. Moffett's set-up demonstrates the advantages of using a rack with a large-scale kit, where curved and straight components are joined into a cage, with support at any angle and suspended cymbals overhead. 'Sugarfoot' Moffett is a powerful showman known for his flashy cymbal playing and 'sweet' footwork, perfect for the touring work he does with Madonna, Cameo and Janet Jackson.

Sleishman Twin pedal (right)

Australian Don Sleishman designed this remarkable pedal way back in 1965. Unfortunately it weighed a ton and was as impractical as Trixon's contemporary oddity, the Speedfire, forcing drummers to sit centrally and square-on to the bass drum. In the mid 1990s the older and wiser Sleishman custom-builds superb drums with his patented 'Suspended Shell' system.

Noonan 5x13 snare drum 1996

(left) Custom-made high quality drums have become increasingly popular in the 1990s. British maker Gary Noonan built this gold-plated heavy gauge brass snare drum, spun in the same manner as the classic American Black Beautys.

Peavey Bobby Rock Renaissance Man kit

(right) Following multi-platinum success with Nelson and the After The Rain album in 1991, Rock has undertaken long clinic tours for Peavey. Peavey created a stir with their new 'Radial Bridge' drums in 1994, pointing out that conventional drums lack an acoustic bridge, and that the 'soundboard' (the shell) is stifled by the hardware mounted on it. Peavey's design transfers the stress onto the heavy wooden 'Radial Bridge' and allows the three-ply maple shell to resonate freely. Rock's kit here includes a Gibraltar rack and Sabian cymbals.

Nick Mason (left) Following a long association with Ludwig, Pink Floyd's Nick Mason converted to Drum Workshop (DW), and is shown here with a DW kit featuring a maple-shell brass edge snare drum. DW's 5000 bass pedals set the industry standard during the late 1970s, and DW started making drums in the 1980s. By the 1990s they'd become the most successful modern American drum company. The drums are recognisable by their Camco-style 'turret' lugs. Each 'timbre matched' six-ply maple shell is individually stamped with its fundamental pitch, and is available in a vast choice of finishes.

77

Mike Portnoy 1995 (above) Portnoy was quickly labelled a potential successor to Neil Peart's throne when Dream Theater's album Images And Words (right) was released in 1992. He kept the spirit of progressive rock alive with his extensive Mapex and Sabian touring kit. Mapex advanced

rapidly following their appearance in 1989. By the mid-1990s they had an impressive endorser list and a broad line of drums, from the entry-level Venus, through the Mars-Pro with Isolated Tom System (ITS), and on to the Mapletech Orion with six-ply maple shells in lacquer or natural waxed finishes.

Paul Geary's Custom Mapex kit c1994 (above) Geary was a member of Extreme when he had this kit custom made for their support slot with Bon Jovi. The six-ply maple shells (16x22, 11x13, 16x16, 6½x14) are dramatically covered in genuine black and white Holstein cowhide.

larger-than-life performers. The magnitude of the modern music scene has attracted and inspired superbly skilled players in all areas of music. The metal scene gave us veterans like Alex van Halen and Tommy Aldridge (Black Oak Arkansas, Whitesnake) and newcomers like Lars Ulrich and Dave Lombardo (Slayer, Grip Inc). Then there have been crossover artists such as Rod Morgenstein (Dixie Dregs, Winger) and Simon Phillips, and solo artists like the Australian Virgil Donati and Terry Bozzio. These are all monster players who warrant a *big* platform.

In fact Bozzio was the first drummer I saw who could duplicate with his feet whatever he played with his hands. Well, almost. Which gives me a link into bass drum pedals. The bass drum pedal has evolved to take as much if not considerably more punishment than every other part of the kit. Starting in the 1960s, players who grew up using the classic Ludwig Speed King, Rogers Swiv-O-Matic, (French) Asba Caroline, Gretsch Floating Action, or – in Keith Moon's case – the rubber-footplated Premier 250, ended up with their roadies raiding the drum store in every town they visited and stuffing flight cases full of as many pedals and spare parts as they could find. The metal or leather straps snapped, the footplates cracked, and springs and bearings exploded.

The modern era of rugged bass pedals started in the early 1970s when Al Duffy began converting Camco pedals to chain-and-sprocket drives. Duffy, you'll remember, customised gear for Billy Cobham. The Camco tools and dies were sold to Drum Workshop in 1979 and they swiftly followed up with their chain drive pedal, the DW 5000C. This was a great success, and chain drives have become the most popular type of pedal today. Cobham also took the idea to Tama, who had bought the Camco name, which is why you'll find the (modified) Camco pedal in Tama catalogues.

THE IRON COBRA

Many drummers who developed double bass drum licks through the 1980s didn't want to carry around two bass drums. The answer was the double pedal, another old idea whose time had come. DW had extended their 5000 to the 5002 double pedal in 1983, again setting the pattern. The other companies busied themselves converting their pedals to doubles. DW in its role as independent hardware company also helped fill the gap

left by the demise of Walberg & Auge. Other independent hardware companies also sprang up, notably Gibraltar who successfully introduced low-cost quality rack systems followed by a complete line of stands and pedals.

Today's heavy pedals have cast footboards ribbed for strength, sprocketed cam action drives, and single or double chains. Beaters are made in different shapes and sizes from various materials – felt, wood or Plexiglas – while Pearl's Power Shifters have four-way beaters in felt and plastic, and Tama's Iron Cobras offer wood, felt or rubber. Sonor were one of the earliest companies to make super-sturdy pedals with three choices of spring strength and a height-adjustable base. Today, all manner of adjustments in stroke, weight and tension can be made to fine-tune your pedal to your technique.

SONOR BOWS TO FASHION

Sonor of Germany is the oldest surviving major modern drum company, dating back to 1875. But Sonor's modern standing as the manufacturer of the most sumptuous of drums seemed to come out of nowhere around the beginning of the 1980s.

While Trixon were big news in the early 1960s, Sonor were almost invisible. Yet The Surfaris' drummer in America is pictured with a Sonor kit way back in 1963 at the time of their immortal hit 'Wipe Out', the perennially dippy surfing instrumental that launched a million school-desk drummers.

By 1969 Sonor was endorsed in the States by major jazz drummers Connie Kay of The Modern Jazz Quartet and Sonny Payne of The Count Basie Orchestra. Yet contemporary issues of the American jazz magazine *Down Beat* still felt justified in describing Sonor as "obscure German drums". As the West German economy rocketed, so Sonor's reputation grew. David Garibaldi played Sonor in the mid 1970s with Tower of Power. Steve Smith of Journey became a Sonor endorser and still is, along with session king Bernard 'Pretty' Purdie, the awesome groover who can be heard on the hits of Aretha Franklin and a hundred others.

Although Sonor had always aimed first for quality, it was with the Signature series of 1980 that they really hit the mark. It was quite the heaviest production kit ever, with mighty twelve-ply beech shells (about half an inch thick). Sonor pointed out in their lavish catalogues that the drum shell "is acoustically passive" and that the head is the "sound generator and acoustic projecting element". In order to assist maximum head vibration, Sonor said, the shell should be massive and not flex. This all seemed to be pretty convincing stuff... but unfortunately the fickle world of fashion dictated that during the 1980s drum shells would get thinner.

Thin shells don't project the fundamental deep tones so well as thick shells, but they do accentuate the highs. And the trend was toward a brighter sounding drum. So Sonor, whatever their oscilloscopes might tell them, had no option but to produce a thinner-shelled drum. This they did in great style with the beautiful birch Sonorlite.

Sonor bowed to fashion once more in the late 1980s with the maple-shelled Hi-Lite which featured tube lugs, rubber insulators and Sonor's Advanced Projection System. Tube lugs became a feature of their mid and budget drum lines, the Force 3000, 2000 and 1000, which despite getting cheaper by the series surprisingly maintained Sonor's rigorous standards.

The heavyweight Signature line has lately been replaced by the Designer, the most extravagant production drums in the world. The Designer hardware is colossal and yet elegant. 'Designer' refers to the fact that you can choose any finish, shell type (birch, maple light or heavy) and configuration (up to three depths for each diameter), an example of the way quality drum marketing is headed.

PREMIER PUNK

When Ringo went with Ludwig in 1963 it wasn't so much a kick in the teeth for Premier as an inevitable sign of the times. Repressed British youth finally got their hands on cool American gear. Luckily there was enough business generated by the Beatles boom for Premier to prosper over the next decade. In fact Premier moved to its (present) purpose-built modern factory in 1977, just as the new Japanese companies began to gather on the horizon.

Like Sonor, Premier had always had a quirky determination to go their own way... and it's nearly been their downfall on more than one occasion. They stuck with flush-braced lugs, flush-base Lokfast stands (which were still offered in the 1981 catalogue alongside tripod Trilok stands), thin shells with reinforcing rings, and die-cast rims, until it was almost curtains. The funny thing is that all these features – except the stands – have now come back into fashion.

One of Premier's most unusual and successful kits was the Resonator. The resonator idea was conceived by Alan Gilby of Richmo drums of Stoke on Trent in the north Midlands. Gilby fitted a thin wooden lining inside Kenny Clare's Ludwig bass drum, giving it a smooth interior and a double shell with a gap between. The resulting increase in volume and projection left their jaws slackened and the idea was sold to Premier.

The Resonator impressed quite a few American players in the 1970s, including Little Feat's Richie Hayward, the Good Rats' Joe Franco, and Clem Burke who with Blondie appropriately played a yellow glitter Resonator kit. Premier's top American endorser, since 1984, has been the brilliant left-hander Rod Morgenstein, of Dixie Dregs and Winger. In the mid 1980s Morgenstein played a Resonator with shells of customised weather-beaten copper finish.

Keith Moon also made his final recordings using a single bass drum Resonator. Moon's devotion to Premier was always a great boost for the company. Premier did him proud with a series of special kits, the 1968 'Pictures Of Lily' kit being the most memorable. They also made a Kenny Clare Resonator kit covered in real Royal Stewart tartan cloth for Kenney Jones in 1974 when he was with Rod Stewart and The Faces.

During the punk era of the late 1970s British drummers like Rat Scabies of The Damned and Rick Buckler of The Jam played Premier. But come the 1980s many British drummers defected to the Japanese companies, just as they had to the American companies in the 1960s. On top of which the Linn drum machine arrived, followed by the Simmons electronic kit. Premier were close to going under.

ECONOMICS AND PREMIER

Promotions manager Roger Horrobin was with Premier from the 1960s through to 1996. In 1987 Premier was saved from a pitiful decline by Yamaha. Horrobin describes the situation before the takeover. "All of a sudden the whole world was hit by recession – the oil crisis and so on. The world became one marketplace, and at that point it changed and wasn't any longer a matter of parochial family businesses. It became very much an international scene."

As Ludwig, Gretsch and Slingerland had in the States, and as Sonor would in 1991, Premier underwent the final break from the old world of family dynasties into the modern world

Paul Weller (right) rose to fame during the British punk movement of the late 1970s with his mod-styled power trio The Jam, enjoying four number one hits starting with 'Going Underground' (1980). Always an intelligent songwriter, Weller has repeated his success a generation later with several critically acclaimed solo albums in the 1990s, including Wildwood and Stanley Road (inset right). Drummer Steve White joined Weller as a precocious 17-year-old in 1983 and together they've developed a rapport that enables them to explore a wide variety of soulful, rhythmic styles. White spends his Weller down-time recording jazz and groove albums and is a valued clinician for Pearl and Sabian.

Steve White's Pearl Masters kit (right; see also front, opposite) This is Steve White's current Pearl Masters Custom maple kit in gold glitter (with the steel rims, tension bolts and lugs plated with 24-carat gold). The kit was specially made in 1995 for White, who comments: "I've sold enough albums with Paul Weller. I deserve it!" The kit consists of a 16x22 bass drum, 11x13 and 16x16 toms, and a 6½x14 snare. White's cymbals are all Sabian HHs: 14" Dark Hats; 16", 18" Rock Crashes, and a 20" Classic Ride. Pedals are from Pearl's DW5000 series, and heads are Aquarian Satin Finish batters with Aquarian lightweight transparents on the bottoms.

RIMS mount (above) The small tom on White's kit is suspended by a RIMS mount which attaches to the lug bolts. White prefers this to Pearl's Integrated Suspension System which attaches to the drum's rim. Single-mounted toms are again fashionable today, allowing closer positioning of the ride cymbal.

Chad Smith (right) Smith possesses a wicked right-foot technique, and mixes funk/rap with grunge/rock in the Red Hot Chili Peppers, as heard on their multi-platinum *Blood Sugar Sex Magik* album (1991). Smith endorses Sabian cymbals, and plays a customised Pearl Masters kit. Typical of the mid 1990s is the compact set-up seen here with a relatively small number of toms.

Pearl Masters Custom Gold snare (below) This has a one-piece solid maple shell, but without reinforcing rings. All metalwork is 24-carat gold-plated. The bridge lugs reduce the metal-to-wood contact. Note the use of white nylon Lug Locks on the tension bolts to prevent tension-slipping.

Steve White's Pearl Masters kit (front, above) Pearl Masters Custom drums are state-of-the-art for the mid 1990s. The vintage-style shells are four-ply maple with proportional four-ply reinforcement glue rings and slightly rounded 45-degree bearing edges. Pearl also offer the Masters Studio as a birch-shelled option, as well as the Masters Extra with six-ply shells minus the reinforcing rings.

of accountants and corporate ownership. "When we went into receivership in 1984 the business would either have been bought in small parts, or nobody would have bought it at all. We saved ourselves by doing a management [leveraged] buyout," Horrobin explains. However, three years later the banks put in their own man, Tony Doughty, "to see what he could make of the company and maybe find a buyer for it". Although Doughty had no knowledge of the percussion business, he found Yamaha.

"We were under-capitalised and couldn't develop things the way we wanted to," Horrobin continues. "Yamaha put in a lot of money and came in permanently, probably thinking we could be a European manufacturing base for their products as well as our own. But they didn't interfere with Premier at all. There were only one or two Japanese managers here looking after the Yamaha product. They didn't put 'Yamaha' on the building or on the letter-heads. They brought in the equipment and the expertise to make their drums.

"The first kit we made for them was the budget Yamaha Power V. They sent a sample kit in November and we had to have it tooled up and ready for the marketplace by the following February. They invested in us to enable us to produce their stuff better. Yamaha benefited and so did we."

Unexpectedly, Yamaha departed in 1993, leaving Premier in a healthier position than they had been since the early 1960s. According to Horrobin, the new kits – Signia and Genista – were enabled by the technology. "The quality of the finish is probably the most significant thing," says Horrobin. "The shells are rounder with better bearing edges due to the Yamaha shell manufacturing process. But we continued our own way with thin shells and reinforcing rings. Our stands hadn't been the best, and that was solved by the Yamaha stands. We also made the Yamaha 9000 for Europe. The same birch was used for the 9000 as for the Premier kits. We were going to have two drum lines, the Yamaha going down one and the Premier down the other, but we didn't achieve that.

"Everything about Yamaha was totally positive," concludes Horrobin. "With the investment they'd made, and what we'd been able to do while they were here, we had the Signia (1992) and almost the Genista (1994). The market changed in our favour and we're on a roll upwards. And we've been able to add to that now with the budget XPK and APK kits."

I always thought that if Premier had made a Rolls Royce kit the British rock stars would have embraced it. Perhaps it took until the post-Yamaha era for this to become a reality. The Signia, with its thin maple shells and traditional Premier beech reinforcing rings, and the Genista, with Yamaha-influenced straight birch shells, are quite unlike anything Premier have produced before, a complete style makeover. British drummers are taking Premier seriously again. There have been a few steadfast supporters like Charlie Morgan, and today you can add to the list players such as Nicko McBrain of Iron Maiden, Jeff Rich of Status Quo, Pete Riley of Jan Cyrka and Tommy Cunningham of Wet Wet Wet.

WORLD DRUMS

The international drum scene is still dominated by Japanese and Far Eastern products. However, the north Americans are gradually winning back some ground and are market leaders in cymbals (Zildjian and Sabian) and drum heads (Remo, Evans and Aquarian). As we've just seen, Europe is represented internationally by the drums of Premier and Sonor (who also produce their own drum heads) and by the cymbals of Paiste (made in Switzerland), Meinl (Germany), Ufip (Italy) and Istanbul (Turkey).

During the 1980s Australian bands like AC/DC and INXS made an international breakthrough, as on a smaller scale did the Australian drum maker Brady who introduced us to wonderful indigenous species of eucalyptus wood like jarrah and wandoo. Aaron Comess of the American band Spin Doctors has a complete kit in ten-ply jarrah. Brady have also popularised solid-block snare drum construction in unusual sizes, such as the 8x12 snare used by ex-Pearl Jam drummer Dave Abbruzzese.

Because of the industry-wide use of maple and birch, as well as Philippine 'mahogany' (red lauan) at the cheap end, it's easy to forget that just about every type of hardwood has been used for drum making in the past. Sonor has used bubinga and beech, Tama has used rosewood and cordia, and years ago Leedy used walnut.

Aside from Brady, two other new and very different companies have become familiar in the 1990s. They illustrate the problem for any new drum company: how do you make inroads and at the same time establish an identity? Drummers, it seems, are pretty conservative when it comes to the form of their drums. The amplifier company Peavey found this out when they decided on a radical look for their 1990s drums. Peavey started by asking why the conventional drum doesn't have a 'bridge' like other acoustic percussion instruments. Their answer was to develop a drum where the tensioning apparatus is mounted on a 'radial bridge' which is separate from the sound chamber (in other words, the shell). This way the shell is free-floating and not constricted by conventional fittings. Peavey are not the only ones to have explored this area. The Australian Dan Sleishman spent years working on his patented Suspended Shell system, where the only contact the shell makes is with the heads. However, Peavey have had the financial muscle to persevere with and develop their product, and the result is indeed some great sounding drums. Whether Peavey can in fact convert a sizeable number of drummers to play something which doesn't look like the average drum remains to be seen.

Mapex, the fourth oriental giant, didn't arrive until 1989. They have the opposite problem: they are not different enough. They started out looking like poor copies of Tama, which is not surprising since they took on Billy Cobham as their main adviser. It's hard to imagine that Mapex can ever have the impact that the Big Three had in the late 1970s, and until they take a few risks they will have an identity problem.

The 1996 Mapex Mapletech Orion series is a superb state-of-the-art drum kit, with some nice design touches, but it looks just like the Yamaha Custom Maple series, with similar low-mass button lugs. Still, at the time of writing Mapex do have endorsers who cover every area of modern music, from Mike Palmer with the number one country singer Garth Brooks, to Herlin Riley, the musical drummer with the world's most popular jazz star, Wynton Marsalis.

HEAD HUNTING

With the return to brighter sounds, the double-ply heads of the 1980s — the Pinstripes and Evans Hydraulics — lost ground to the more resonant Ambassadors. Although Remo still has the lion's share of the market there is now a tantalising choice of alternatives. Aside from the in-house products of Premier, Ludwig and Sonor, which are mostly only used by players of those particular makes of drums, the major independents are

Evans, Aquarian and, recently, Attack. Evans underwent a radical facelift when they changed their soft, composite rims to a hi-tech aluminium computer-aided design in the late 1980s. The single-ply Evans Resonant heads in bright colours and their white coated Uno 58s have a feel of real quality about them, with accurately formed and distinctively high, squared collars. Evans' Genera EQ two-head bass drum system led the way back towards more rounded bass drum sounds after years of the pillow-stuffed thud.

In the 1990s the Aquarian company of ex-big band star and Rogers clinician Roy Burns offers another distinctive line of heads. Aquarian also have a special collar design, called Sound Curve, which they claim is vital to the tuning integrity of the heads. From early 1996 Aquarian has used a new formulation X-R (Extra Resonance) Mylar, and their extended line now covers everything from Satin Finish thin single-ply heads to Impact bass drum heads which require no muffling.

MULTIPLYING CYMBALS

The average music fan would be astonished to discover that the humble cymbal exists in a hundred varieties. I doubt if anyone – even in the late 1970s – could have predicted that so many variations would be wrought from flat discs of bronze. Every trick in the book of modern metallurgy is called upon to tease out further subtleties of tone.

It's all pushed along by the keen rivalry between the triad of major companies – Zildjian, Sabian and Paiste – with added competition from Meinl, Ufip, Istanbul and others. They all continue to diversify, and choice is so great as to be bewildering. In fact most cymbals still fall into the basic categories of ride, crash, hi-hat, effects and China types. The reason there are so many is that every type of music and player, at beginner, intermediate and pro levels, is represented by one line or more.

While Zildjian have brought the traditional K sound into the modern era with their K Customs, Paiste have gone the other way and adapted their modern 'secret' alloy to re-create sounds from the 1940s-1960s in their Traditional line. Both Zildjian with their A Customs and Sabian with their AAXs have further enhanced their biggest selling lines. And all three companies have greatly improved their mid-price B8 lines: Paiste's Alpha, Zildjian's Edge, and Sabian's Pro. On the effects and exotic side a recent trend is towards 'Latin' cymbals – Sabian El Sabors and Zildjian Azukas.

Back in Europe, Meinl adapted the wavy outline of Paiste's Sound Edge hi-hat in their Lightning crashes. And in Turkey a group of ex-K Zildjian workers established the Istanbul company in the early 1980s. They work on a small scale in the traditional way, and turn out some great cymbals reminiscent of the old Ks, but a little more modern and bright. Just recently, in a split reminiscent of Zildjian and Sabian, the Istanbul camp has divided and a new line of similar looking high quality cymbals has arrived called Bosphorus.

The other home of cymbals is Italy. Today the co-operative cymbal makers of Pistoia make Ufip Earcreated cymbals – emphasising the primacy of the human ear in their evaluation. The Class line is made by a unique roto-casting method and is easily comparable with the best from any of the other manufacturers. Ufip has increased its lines to include the dark earthy Naturals and the penetrating Rough series with 'microfine' grooving.

BACK TO KRUPA: RETRO KITS

From Gene Krupa on throughout the entire history of jazz and rock the four- or five-piece drum kit has reigned. A peak of sorts was reached during the late 1980s when some drummers built up massive kits. But during the 1990s the trend has been to scale back down again.

The virtues of a simple approach with a basic kit, and 'playing for the song', have influenced this drift. For some drummers and bands this was always the way. But the current movement owes much to the umpteenth revival of guitar-based rock typified by the success of Guns N'Roses, with drummer Matt Sorum, around the turn of the 1990s. Following on from Guns N' Roses were the grunge bands, with drummers such as Dave Abbruzzese, who played with Pearl Jam, and Dave Grohl of Nirvana.

In Britain the basic kit has been the mainstay, from the punks of the late 1970s through the indie (alternative) bands of the 1980s and on to the 1990s Britpop groups who openly shout their 1960s influences. In late 1996 four-piece kits – sometimes actual renovated 1960s kits – are the cool thing to play. Alan White recorded the most influential recent British rock album, Oasis' *What's The Story, Morning Glory* (1995) on a 1960s

Rogers kit he bought for £250 [$400] while working in Foote's, the London drum store. There is a small but significant international industry that unearths classic drum kits from the 1950s to the 1970s, many of which still sound great – or better – 30 or 40 years on.

The main concession to the present era that is likely to be made with vintage kits is in strengthening the hardware and maybe in the adoption of RIMS-type mounting. As we've discovered, all the modern companies seem to have been dodging one another's patents in order to come up with some form of resonance isolation – or simply have been fitting RIMS mounts under licence. Ludwig, for example, reissued the Vintage Super Classic in 1996 in non-power sizes and with recommended RIMS mounts.

Another reason for the move to smaller kits was that during the 1980s many acts included a percussionist as well as or instead of a kit drummer. The drummer was called upon to keep the groove – only necessitating a small kit – while the percussionist had free reign. Percussion blossomed like never before and nowadays if anyone's got a massive set-up and a rack it's likely to be the percussionist. Certainly the conclusion for most small-time drummers is that racks are less convenient than stands.

Along with the fad for 1960s drums has come the rediscovery of glittery, pearly and gaudy plastic finishes. These are steadily replacing the regulation lacquered finishes of the 1980s. And there's also the hint of a return to non-power sizes. Adding weight to this trend is the influence of key players like Dennis Chambers who regularly played shallower sizes. (Chambers was the 'P-funk' movement's preferred drummer, and went on to a variety of jazz-rock work with John Scofield, the Brecker Brothers and John McLaughlin, among others.) Maybe drummers should also brace themselves for a reaction against another 1980s affectation, 1920s-style tubular pipe lugs, which are, let's face it, a very un-1960s look.

It may be flattering for the American companies to see their history revered by this latest return to vintage kits and vintage looks, but it doesn't do their sales any good, nor that of the Japanese. The popularity of four-piece kits is also not good for sales when five-piece kits had long been standard and drummers were expected to graduate to six- and seven-piece kits as they moved up the ladder.

SIGNATURE SNARES

While drummers have been cutting down on the number of tom toms, they've been getting more and more into multiple-choice snare drums – often a combination of the vintage and the new. Star 'signature' snare drums are nothing new, but they presented the Japanese with one solution to the predicament of their unpopular snare drums. In 1996 Yamaha released no less than six Steve Gadd signature snare drums, in birch, maple, steel and brass.

Every big star is lining up for their very own signature snare drum. There are already dozens to mull over, in every material, size and type of construction. The choice is fabulous; the problem is how to pick one. They're generally made in small runs so they're expensive, and it follows that the average drummer could easily make a costly mistake.

This is the down-side of having more and more choices. The up-side is that everyone can now achieve individuality – even with a minimal kit – via the increasing options for customisation. Every combination of finish, size, hardware and snare drum a drummer could want is offered. After that, why not splash out on customised paint jobs, exotic veneers or, for the really flash, gold-plated hardware?

From the mid 1990s there was a slight indication that the 20-year Japanese stronghold on the commercial market might be slipping a little. This has to do with the moves in fashion back to classic American drums that I've just outlined, combined with the progress of companies like DW, Remo, Premier and Sonor. It's also because modern drum kits are now so well made that there is simply less need to be changing every few years. In this respect the Japanese (and other) companies are the victims of their own success. A quality modern drum kit is likely to be a major investment which will last a very long time.

I've managed to get this far in the book without mentioning electronic kits. I'm only bringing up the subject here because I wanted to say that throughout the 1980s I feared the acoustic drum kit's time was limited, in the same way that the acoustic piano has been largely outstripped by electronic keyboards. I still think the acoustic kit may lose its dominant place to electronics some time in the future, but during the 1990s the drum kit has made a surprising recovery, while electronic kits are a rare sight, on the live stage at least. No one knows what's coming next. But certainly the drum kit is in a very healthy state. It hardly needs saying, but I'll say it anyway: the choice of drums, cymbals, heads and hardware is greater in the 1990s than it ever has been.

AND FINALLY... MUSIC

I said at the beginning of this book that the art of playing the drum kit is in a continuing state of development. The best rock drummers are world-class virtuosi who take the drum kit every bit as seriously as any classical concert pianist or major jazz saxophonist. And yet few beyond the paying customers at drum clinics know or care, and fewer still would believe you if you told them so. Vinnie Colaiuta is a rhythmical genius, did you say? "Who's Vinnie Colaiuta," replies the man in the street.

Today the virtuoso rock drummer – all fired up with a million licks, rhythmic tricks and illusions – gets it off his or her chest through the medium of the drum clinic, something that used to be educational but is now often closer to a gladiatorial contest, a minor branch of the sporting industry.

In the mid 1990s Terry Bozzio performed solo percussion concerts on the extended drum kit. Bozzio has the audacity and the honesty to stand up and say: 'This is my instrument and this is the music I play on it.' I'd love to see other great kit players follow Bozzio's lead. How else will they be taken as seriously as an Evelyn Glennie?

But this also highlights the dilemma. During the seminal years when rock took off internationally, from the mid 1960s to the late 1970s, original creative players were also pop stars, from Ginger Baker to John Bonham and right up to Stewart Copeland. The implication is that while ability on the kit advances unstoppably, it has actually surpassed what is required to play commercial rock music. Today virtuosity invariably finds a home in HM or progressive rock, entertaining genres where a bit of showing off is appreciated and expected. These are the areas inhabited by the instrumental pollwinners and reviled by the critics.

Through the 1980s and the 1990s, amazingly athletic players have emerged, technically sophisticated way beyond the heroes of earlier times. Some are hugely successful and give great pleasure. We all have our favourites. I just look forward to the day when one of them becomes a household name as famous as Gene Krupa or Ringo Starr.

DRUM DIRECTORY

DRUM DIRECTORY

There follows a series of short biographical introductions to the major drum companies and many of the smaller drum companies mentioned in the main text, arranged here in alphabetical order of company name. Because there is so much to say about the drum companies there was not space in this directory to include the cymbal and head manufacturers, although they are of course discussed in the main text.

AJAX

At the start of the rock era in Britain in the mid/late 1950s, Ajax drums were second to Premier though in rather smaller numbers. The Ajax name had first appeared in 1927 on drums manufactured by Hawkes & Son (London) Ltd. This was soon after the visit of George Way from America, drumming up European business for Leedy, and early Ajax drums show a keen awareness of Leedy and Ludwig & Ludwig designs. Hawkes combined with Boosey & Co in 1930 to become Boosey & Hawkes Ltd, the company which manufactured Ajax drums right through to 1970 before giving up the unequal struggle with fashionable American imports.

Ajax drums featured die-cast rims and bullet-shaped die-cast lugs. Ajax snare drums were highly regarded and included the Pipper 5 x 14 and 7½ x 14 with a parallel action strainer. The shallow Snapper had a 3"-deep shell with a simpler Ludwig type side lever strainer – a handsome drum which would be considered modern in the 1990s. As well as plain white plastic Ajax drums were available in the usual range of pearls and sparkles.

Ajax made good drums which were played by many of the British jazz stars. However, virtually all the British rockers played Premier and most defected to Ludwig following Ringo. In a last ditch attempt to cash in, Ajax had a complete facelift and launched the Nu Sound line of drums in 1967. With their triple-flanged rims, American-looking lugs and mounted 12" and 13" toms they were rather more modern than Premier at the time. But they were still no match for the American drums, and Ajax disappeared around 1970. Ajax also marketed their own brand of cheap cymbals and Impact plastic heads.

The five-piece Nu Sound Forte kit offered mounted 8 x 12 and 9 x 13 sizes, with a 12 x 22 bass drum, while the four-piece Staccato had a 14 x 20 bass 0drum. Stands had old fashioned flush-based 'mike stand' bases, but there was a modern twin spring Accelerator bass drum pedal.

From the mid/late 1950s through to the mid 1960s Boosey also produced Edgware and Stratford drums. These started out as budget versions of Ajax but ended up being very similar. Premier's Roger Horrobin says that Ajax, and probably Edgware, were actually made by Premier at some stage. During the 1960s Boosey also made Rogers drums under license, which most likely diluted their efforts regarding Ajax. After 1970 the Boosey & Hawkes drum division continued only as distributors of Beverley drums, by then made by Premier.

ASBA

Asba stainless steel drums, made in France, were quite well known in Britain during the 1970s along with their progressive and much copied cam-action Caroline bass drum pedal. Asba also made conventional wood shell drums and Perspex drums along with most others, but with the coming of the Japanese, Asba disappeared at the start of the 1980s.

AUTOTUNE

Arbiter Autotune drums were introduced in 1975, made in Britain. They originally had fibreglass shells with a screw-down 'pickle jar' tension system which Ivor Arbiter says was inspired by the design of his wife's pressure cooker. Jazz-rock drummer Jon Hiseman, as well as Carl Palmer, helped with the design.

The shells had a greater diameter than the heads giving them a similar appearance to the vintage American Duplex drums. There was only one tuning lug per shell and this was tuned by a special ratchet which enabled tuning of both the top and bottom heads from the same sitting position. Originally they were supplied with the Rogers Swiv-O-Matic tom holder and bass pedal, Rogers Supreme hi hat and Rogers Samson double braced cymbals stands.

The Autotune Rock 100 outfit was a five-piece kit with standard sizes available in Pure White or Pure Black. Later Autotune drums were made using wood shells coated on the inside with the same white paint as Arbiter's Hayman drums (which Autotune superseded, albeit with rather less success). For the brief time Autotune drums were around they were played by many British stars including Dave Mattacks of Fairport Convention, Tony Newman of Sounds Incorporated, and Graeme Edge of The Moody Blues.

AYOTTE

Ray Ayotte is based in Vancouver, Canada, and specialises in custom making drum kits of the highest quality. Endorsers include Matt Cameron of Sound Garden. Ayotte drums have a very distinctive look due to their TuneLock lugs which

have an easy-release flip-over 'T' hook design. For an even more distinctive look kits can also be supplied with wooden hoop rims all around – not just on the bass drums.

Ayotte started out selling drums from his Drums Only store in 1972, quickly becoming the biggest retailer in Vancouver. The business also included repairs and custom-building. Later in the decade Ayotte was buying Camco drums from Los Angeles and adding hardware and tom holders. He started to custom build his own drums from 1983.

Ayotte shells, which can be ordered in any reasonable depth, are made from six-ply rock maple from eastern Canada and the US. Maple reinforcing hoops ('sound rings') are fitted once the shell has been cut to size. Snare drums are anything up to 30-ply, and they've even tried a 50-ply. For the hard hitter who still wants some warmth, 18-ply is a good compromise. The special rack-and-pinion snare release is another Ayotte exclusive. Beautiful stain and lacquer finishes are painstakingly achieved and include sunburst, metallic, Ebony Satin and Red Marble. Ayotte also manufacture fibreglass drums based on the 1970s British Staccato drums.

BEVERLEY

Beverley is a town in north-east England with a long history of musical instrument manufacturing, including the making of drums. The Beverley drum operation was bought by Premier in 1957, although the Beverley factory

continued to work as a separate entity. Beverley was a familiar name in Britain through the 1960s and 1970s, and ads in *Melody Maker* in 1969, for example, offered the Panorama 21 five-piece kit as well as the Panorama 22 seven-piece double-bass-drum kit that featured a 21 metal snare and a choice of 14 finishes. During the 1970s there was the Beverley Galaxy kit. After Boosey & Hawkes discontinued the Ajax name in 1970, Premier supplied them with the Beverley line. During the mid to late 1970s Premier also supplied Rosetti with Hamma drums which were similar to Beverley.

BRADY

Chris Brady has custom made snare drums from the mid 1980s in Australian hardwoods. Bass drums and toms are fashioned from ten plies of jarrah, an extremely hard species of eucalyptus wood. It's bent under extreme pressure rather than steamed. The tom shells are ¼" thick, the bass drums ⅜" thick. The chromed lugs are of solid brass and the square-size rack toms are fitted with RIMS. Finishes include natural satin, cherry red gloss, black gloss, walnut stain, piano white, white or silver gimlet.

Brady also makes block-construction snares from wandoo (including a 7x12 'soprano') and from jarrah ply (a 6½x14). Chad Smith of Red Hot Chili Peppers has a 5x14 jarrah snare, while Aaron Comess of The Spin Doctors has a jarrah kit with 22" bass, 8", 10", 14" and 16" toms, and piccolo and 5" snares.

CANNON

Cannon Percussion of Ohio produce Attack drumheads which have come to the fore in the mid 1990s and are used by Gerry Brown with Stevie Wonder and Michael Bland with Prince.

CAPELLE

During the 1970s, the French company Capelle marketed Orange drums which, like Asba, were of good quality with some interesting features. The metal snare drum had a sophisticated Dynasonic-type parallel action metal frame supporting the snare and giving snare response right over the bearing edges. The snare head could be changed without altering the snare setting. The hi-hat – still known as the Charleston, a label from back in the 1920s and 1930s – had spring tension adjustment high up the stand so it could be applied without stooping. And the bass pedal was mounted on a variable length vertical post attached to the top and bottom bass drum hoop so that the pedal could be adjusted for height and tilt. The pedal folded flat to be packed away still attached to the bass drum hoop. This is actually a development from the way pedals were mounted in the days before Ludwig's 1909 floor pedal. Capelle Orange Turbo drums with an enormously elongated bass drum were first exhibited at the 1982 NAMM musical instruments trade show in the US.

90

CARLTON

Carlton is one of the great names of British pre-rock drums, dating back to 1935. During the early rock period Carlton produced pop, orchestral and 'Gaelic' military drums. The President line was semi-pro, while Gigster was for the beginner. Carlton also made their own Symara and marketed Rassem cymbals during the 1950s at less than a third of the price of the Turkish 'K' Zildjians which they also sold.

During the 1960s Carlton made the Big Beat, which was a five-piece kit plus a pair of bongos – a glance back in the dance band direction. The Carlton Continental kit included the 3" Cracker piccolo snare, still popular in 1967. The kits were available in various pearl, glitter and wave finishes.

Carlton managed to find a handful of rock endorsers including Ric Rothwell of Wayne Fontana & the Mindbenders, and top session player Bobby Graham who played on many mid 1960s beat group hits including some Kinks tracks. Also playing Carlton was Micky Waller (with organist Brian Auger), and Britain's first female drumming chart star, Anne 'Honey' Lantree of The Honeycombs (who's still playing with The Honeycombs in the mid 1990s, incidentally).

CORDER

Jim Corder started the Corder Drum Company of Alabama when he bought the tooling apparatus, dies and moulds from the defunct Fibes company in 1978. Horrified at the mess and potential health

hazards of producing fibreglass shells, he produced maple wood shell drums with Fibes fittings and mounts from around 1981 through to 1990. (See also DARWIN.)

DALLAS

John E Dallas and Sons Ltd of London was established in 1875. During the early 1920s they marketed Jedson drums which were actually made by Premier and others. Dallas started to make their own Carlton drums in 1935, and Dallas merged with Ivor Arbiter to form Dallas-Arbiter in 1968, producing the successful Hayman drum line. Arbiter parted with Dallas in the early 1970s, Hayman withered and Dallas was wound up in 1975. (See also GIGSTER.)

DARWIN

Ken Austin was in artist relations with Pearl before he took over the Corder/Fibes line in 1990 and produced Darwin drums in the US until 1994. Steve Gorman of Black Crowes has played a Corder kit.

DRUM WORKSHOP

Drum Workshop, or DW, has grown from the George Way/Camco tradition, and is the most successful of the new American drum companies.

When Camco dissolved in the mid 1970s, LA drummer Don Lombardi bought the tools and dies for manufacturing the hardware. The first result of this was a patented chain-and-sprocket-drive bass drum pedal, the 5000CX. This pedal was immediately popular and has led to the Turbo 5000T version, with stabilising footboard, and the Accelerator 5000A with offset sprocket for faster playing.

DW also led the way in the move during the 1980s to double pedals, manufacturing double versions of the 5000 series. Many players latched on to them before all the other companies had a chance to develop their own.

DW have followed their success in pedals with equally acclaimed drums made from six-ply maple with six-ply reinforcing rings. Lombardi's partner John Good personally selects and 'timbre matches' shells to make up customised kits. DW were one of the leaders today's customised drum kits, also offering a huge range of over 150 lacquered finishes plus a choice of chrome, brass or black rims, lugs and so on. John Good stamps each shell with its fundamental resonant pitch before it has fittings drilled and the finish applied. DW also produce brass shell snare drums, and brass Edge snare drums with shells which are half brass and half wood.

DW endorsers include Stephen Perkins (Jane's Addiction, Porno For Pyros), Jim Keltner, Jonathan Moffet (Madonna, Michael Jackson), Terry Bozzio, Neil Peart, Sheila E, Tommy Lee (Mötley Crüe), Philip 'Fish' Fisher (Fishbone) and Zak Starkey (The Who).

DUPLEX

Duplex is a name largely lost to history, but it's an important link in the development of the modern drum. Duplex was founded by Emile Boulanger who started making drums around 1882 in St Louis, Missouri, and came up with several important stepping stones to the modern kit before his death in 1908. These included claw-hook tensioners and the first separate-tension snare drum. The company was developed by one Jules Meyer, and during the 1930s Duplex produced unique drums which had aluminium shells but were covered in plastic finishes like wooden drums. The shells had a greater diameter than the rims and the tension bolts actually passed down the inside. This gave them smooth outer shells which looked superficially like British Autotune drums of the 1970s, although the latter had a very different tuning principle. The Duplex company was wound up in 1968.

EAMES

Eames are custom makers of fine drum shells, largely hand crafted. The drums are used by Brazilian percussionist and kit drummer Airto Moreira among others. The roots of Eames go back to the Stone drum company, which was founded in 1890 by percussionist George Burt Stone (father of George Lawrence Stone, the famed rudimental drummer, author and drum maker of Boston, Massachusetts). Around 1949 George Stone sold his drum making equipment to Ralph Eames, one of his pupils, and Eames began his own custom repair shop. In 1972 one of Eames' pupils, Joe MacSweeney, started to work for Eames – mostly making rope tension drums for the American Bicentennial celebrations in 1976. Two years later MacSweeney bought the company.

Eames first made 12-ply ½" shells for bass drums and toms, later producing lighter 9-ply ⅜" shells. The plies are steam bent and laminated one ply at a time. MacSweeney made a 15-ply ⅝" birch snare drum which Danny Gotlieb played with the fusion guitarist Pat Metheny. The drum was based on the classic Stone Master Model snare drum. Gotlieb gave an Eames 7x14 drum to Steve Jordan (Keith Richards, Blues Brothers) who says it's the source of the high pitched snare drum sound that he's noted for.

MacSweeney also restored some old Radio King drums to make up the set which Buddy Rich played from the fall of 1983 through to his death in April 1987. This kit included a 14 x 26 bass drum, although apparently Joe was about to present Rich with a 28" drum that he'd requested.

EDGWARE

see AJAX

FIBES

The Fibes drum company was formed in the middle 1960s by drummer Bob Grauso and drummer/chemist John Morena in Farmingdale, Long Island, New York. Fibes was a pioneer of the fibreglass shell construction movement of the 1970s – and the Fibes shell was probably the best. Virtually indestructible, and impervious to weather, it also had fibreglass reinforcing hoops for

91

added stability. The sound was brilliant and responsive.

Fibes also had some great hardware ideas. One example was the Sta-Way rubber bumper which attaches to the snare drum rim and stops the snare drum from scratching the mounted tom. I've had one for years and I wish I could find some more.

Despite the fading of Fibes in the late 1970s, in a sense they never went away since the distinctive Fibes diamond-shape lugs spent the intervening years adorning Corder drums (1979-90) and Darwin drums (1990-1994). After that, drum store proprietor Tommy Robertson of Austin, Texas, bought the Darwin company, reinstated the name Fibes, and Fibes drums have been available again since 1995. First to appear were snare drums in crystallite (clear acrylic), maple or fibreglass, then full sets in crystallite or maple. The maple drums have Jasper-made six-ply shells, similar to Gretsch.

GIGSTER

Many a British drummer started out on a red glitter Gigster in the late 1950s and early 1960s. Gigster was the basic line in the Dallas Carlton stable. The kits had single headed toms and snare drums which had clip-over single flange hoops – like something left over from the 1930s! They did a great job in getting so many players started, but would be exchanged at the first opportunity for an Olympic or, better still, an Ajax, Stratford or Premier. The 1964 Gigster catalogue lists finishes in white enamel, blue, gold or red glitter.

BILLY GLADSTONE

Billy Gladstone was the original featured percussionist at the Radio City Music Hall in New York. A brilliant man, he was also an inventor and maker of drum equipment. Gretsch Gladstone drums are sought after items from the 1940s. Among his designs is a remote cable hi-hat which was also marketed by Gretsch during the 1940s. Lang Percussion of Brooklyn today manufacture copies of his famous snare drum with three-way tuning which allowed the bottom head to be tensioned separately by the seated drummer in the confines of the theatre pit. The originals are among the most prized collectors items as only about 50 were ever built.

GMS

The GMS drum company is a recent addition to the revived American scene. Founders Rob Mazzella and Tony Gallino produce three lines of drums all with eight-ply maple shells. The Grand Master Series has solid brass tubular lugs and snare mechanism; the Road Series is the same but has a solid plastic finish rather than a painted finish. The CL Classic Lug series has single ended lugs. Endorsers include Bobby Rondinelli of Black Sabbath, Mark Zonder of Fates Warning, David Beyer with Melissa Etheridge and Eric Kretz of Stone Temple Pilots.

GRETSCH

Friedrich Gretsch emigrated to the USA from Germany in 1872 and

set up his musical instrument business in 1883. Friedrich died young and his son Fred, still a teenager, took over in the 1890s. This Fred Gretsch built up the Brooklyn company, supplying drums, banjos and other musical items. By 1916 the Gretsch company was located in its own large building on Broadway, Brooklyn, where it remained until the Gretsch HQ was moved to Cincinnati, Ohio, in 1972.

During the 1930s the Gretsch name was promoted through Chick Webb who played Gretsch Gladstone drums, designed by the Radio City Music Hall percussionist Billy Gladstone. But it was after World War II that Gretsch drums stole the lead. Gretsch had already pioneered the plywood shell during the late 1920s, but in the early 1940s they started to make plywood shells in a new way. This involved staggering the plies so that a strong shell could be made without a single butted or overlapped joint, obviating the need for reinforcing glue rings. Thus the original three-ply straight-wall shells were built. Added to this, Gretsch used heavy die-cast rims while the other manufacturers used either flat section rims, or the triple flanged steel or brass rim (as initiated by the Ludwigs from 1938).

During the late 1940s Gretsch also pioneered the move to smaller size bass drums and convenient hardware such as disappearing bass drum spurs. (Gretsch also later extended these inside the shell to produce the first internal support spurs.) From the early big band days of 28" monsters, sizes had gradually reduced, and Gretsch now started to popularise 20" and even 18" bass drums. These were much easier to transport and also suited the sound of small group jazz which was taking over from big band jazz.

The Gretsch shells went through a four-ply stage before settling at six-ply maple during the 1960s. The thickness of the shells has remained more or less the same throughout, and to this day they have an inner coating of 'secret formula' silver paint. The drums which are most sought after are from the 1950s and 1960s, bearing the Gretsch logo on a 'round badge'. These feature the familiar rounded Broadkaster lug design which has been imitated by many other companies. It's interesting to note that on earlier drums the bearing edges are not the sharp 45-degree type common today. In fact, bearing edges on older drums may slope away from the inner edge (the opposite of today's practice).

The sought-after Gretsches have attained that special drum status occupied by the Radio King and Supraphonic snare drums, a status which transcends logic. Due to some fortuitous and magical combination of craftsmanship and design they are considered to produce a great sound. It's a well known fact that many famous drummers record with Gretsch drums in preference to any other make.

Gretsch were closely associated with the great jazz drummers of the 1950s and 1960s – Elvin Jones, Art Blakey, Mel Lewis and so on – and they were also played by

many rockers, from Elvis's DJ Fontana through to the Stones' Charlie Watts. Gretsch sported some amazing finishes, too, including natural lacquers and stains, plus a wide range of pearls, sparkles and dazzling flames. But from 1967 when Gretsch sold out to Baldwin the name lost some of its magic. The manufacture of the drums moved from Brooklyn to Booneville, Arkansas, in 1970, continuing there until 1981, after which it moved to various Baldwin sites in Arkansas.

Gretsch octagonal-badge drums were available through the 1970s, cosmetically unchanged except in the introduction of concert toms and power sizes. Gretsch steered clear of the fibreglass and Plexiglas fads only venturing as far as producing shells with chrome cladding. However, with the exception of the ever-popular Floating Action bass drum pedal (manufactured by Camco) the hardware started to look seriously dated. Also during the mid 1970s the budget Gretsch Blackhawk line was introduced.

Baldwin went bankrupt in 1983 and in January 1985 Gretsch returned to family ownership with another Fred Gretsch, the nephew of Fred Gretsch Jnr. The company is now located in Savannah, Georgia. Through the 1980s it seemed to languish unchanged, the six-ply maple shells still manufactured by Jasper Wood Products of Indiana, but the hardware lagging behind.

However, certain stalwart endorsers kept the name in the spotlight, most importantly Phil Collins, Tony Williams, and Harvey

Mason (the great studio player who inspired a generation of funk drummers with his stunning performance on Herbie Hancock's 1973 album *Headhunters*). In 1996 Vinnie Colaiuta announced his defection from Yamaha to Gretsch, creating another buzz. With Bissonette on Slingerland and Colaiuta on Gretsch are we seeing the rebirth of the grand old names?

HAYMAN

In 1968 Ivor Arbiter merged with the venerable British drum company John E Dallas to form Dallas Arbiter Ltd. Dallas produced the historic Carlton drums, which were outdated and losing money. Arbiter, who'd had great success importing American drums, decided it was time to produce a British drum which could compete with the Americans. George Hayman drums were introduced in February 1969 and exhibited that August at the London trade show. The first ads to run in *Melody Maker* pictured Mitch Mitchell with a Midnight Blue Big Sound kit and Brian 'Blinky' Davison of The Nice with a Gold Ingot Recording kit with 18" bass drum.

With their white-painted Vibrasonic interiors and thin-walled shells with reinforcing glue rings, Hayman drums copied the American style of makers like Ludwig and Camco. The Hayman kits had Remo heads and a wooden 5½" snare drum with a simple Ludwig-style side-lever strainer. The snare also had ten lugs, American-style, and triple-flanged rims, contrasting with

Premier's Royal Ace snare, for example, which had eight lugs and die-cast rims. The turret lugs were of course copied from the George Way/Camco design, although they were die-cast where the Camco lugs were turned from solid.

The Hayman outfits included the standard Big Sound (with 14x22 bass, 9x13 and 16x16 toms and a 5/12x14 snare) as well as the Showman five-piece (with a choice of 14x22, 14x24 or 15x26 bass drum, plus an extra mounted 8x12 tom. The Pacemaker had a 13x20 bass drum, and the Recording had 'jazz' sizes (12x18 bass drum with 8x12 and 14x14 toms. Lou Dias of Supreme Drums in north-east London had the last few Hayman kits, which included 10x14 toms and rare 6½" wood-shell snare drums. Finishes available were Solid Silver, Gold Ingot, Midnight Blue, Matt Black, Regal Red, Iceberg (see-through) and Natural Pine (laminated veneer).

Hardware included the Speedamatic bass drum pedal with single spring, three speed adjust and wide strap, and Speedamatic hi-hat pedal which had direct pull and (patented) dual external springs.

The single and double shell mount tom holders were unlike anybody else's: very strong but awkward to position and liable to crush your knuckles.

The 1971 brochure pictures the cream of British rock and jazz drummers with Hayman kits, including Aynsley Dunbar (a hugely underrated British drummer who wisely emigrated to LA and played with Frank Zappa and Jefferson Starship), Jon Hiseman, top sessioneer Ronnie Verrall (who as the drummer behind Animal of TV's *The Muppets* would get to spar with Buddy Rich), John Marshall (who played with guitarist John McLaughlin in his pre-Mahavishnu Orchestra days) and Phil Seamen (regarded by his peers as the greatest British jazz drummer).

Hayman was discontinued around 1975. As with many other respected lines an inferior Taiwanese version of Hayman was launched briefly in the late 1980s and early 1990s, and thankfully sank without trace.

IMPACT

Impact is a Wisconsin-based manufacturer of fibreglass drums. The tom toms are square-shaped horns with bottom cutaways so that sound projects forward, as with North drums. The holes and cutaways make them lightweight. The bass and snare drums have conventional shape.

JASPER

Furniture company and ply wood experts based in Jasper, Indiana, who make or have made drum shells for George Way, Camco and Gretsch, among others.

KELLER

Like Jasper, Keller is an independent American shell manufacturing company who've supplied shells to several of the top American drum companies including Rogers, DW and Gretsch.

LANG PERCUSSION

Lang Percussion of Brooklyn produce replicas of the rare three way tuned Billy Gladstone snare drum. Lang snare drums have been played by Billy Cobham and Peter Erskine amongst others.

U.G. LEEDY

Although Leedy drums have passed into history and don't figure much in the story of rock, Ulysses Grant Leedy is an important figure in the early development of the drum kit. During the late 19th century Leedy was a percussionist in Indianapolis. He began manufacturing drums somewhere around 1895, and in line with the times also produced percussion and sound effects. Leedy is credited with inventing the adjustable snare drum stand in 1898.

When the Ludwig brothers started up in 1909 they became the Chicago agents for Leedy equipment. They parted ways with Leedy to make their own brass-shelled snare drums at a time when Leedy preferred wood. Leedy made solid wood snare drums of walnut and maple which are sought after today.

During the 1920s Leedy employed George Way as a salesman. Way visited Europe around 1926 and is said to have influenced European drum making, although the influence no doubt worked both ways. Leedy drums were available in Britain and the Carlton snare drum pictured on page 15 has similar square lugs to Leedy's 1930s box 'X' lugs. The cast lug with the swivel nut is possibly Way's most enduring contribution to modern drum design.

From the beginning of the 1930s Leedy drums were swallowed up by the Conn corporation, as were Ludwig & Ludwig. But while Ludwig eventually regained their name and prospered, the Leedy name was sold to Slingerland in the mid 1950s and was down-graded to a secondary line. The Leedy name continued as a subsidiary of Slingerland until the end of the 1960s but had very little effect on the rock era.

LUDWIG

Ludwig is the most famous American drum company and one of the oldest. William F Ludwig was born in Germany in 1879. His family emigrated to America where William and his ill-fated brother Theobald became highly skilled classical and rudimentary percussionists, working in the Chicago area. The brothers started the Ludwig & Ludwig drum company in 1909. After Theobald's death from flu at the age of 28, William Ludwig Snr continued in the drum business for most of his life, a highly respected, major figure right up to his death in 1973 at the age of 93.

The Ludwigs started out by producing the first workable bass drum pedal, and immediately followed with the first proper snare release. The business did well in the 1920s, peaking around 1926 with sales worth one million dollars. The first Black Beauty engraved brass-shell snare drums

were made around 1927. However, the coming of 'talkie' movies put many percussionists out of work and this, combined with the US stock market crash of 1929, stalled Ludwig's progress.

Ludwig sold the business to the CG Conn corporation of Elkhart, Indiana, in 1929, even though Conn bought Ludwig's main rival, Leedy, around the same time. William Ludwig was supposed to work with Conn but soon became unhappy with the arrangement. From 1937 William branched out on his own again back in Chicago. Joined by his son, William F Ludwig Jnr, he formed the Wm. F. Ludwig Drum Company. However, since Conn owned the Ludwig & Ludwig title the Ludwigs were forced to use a different name. They chose their initials: WFL.

WFL started with the original Speedking footpedal, and around 1938 introduced the stick-saving triple-flanged rim. WFL continued until the mid 1950s when they managed to buy back the Ludwig name from Conn, and the modern Ludwig company was born. At the same time Slingerland also bought themselves back from Conn and took over the old Leedy name. This all coincided with the early days of rock, and Ludwig soon took the lead. Newly invigorated Ludwig steamed ahead, while Slingerland still dithered over the triple-flanged rim and allowed Leedy to stagnate. Elsewhere, Gretsch was coming on strong, particularly with the small jazz groups, while Rogers was just entering its zenith, though on a smaller and more expensive scale than Ludwig.

The Ludwig drums with their thin

three-ply mahogany/poplar shells produced a loud and bright sound with plenty of depth. The updated Speedking pedal came at the beginning of the 1950s, with arched rocker shaft and wider footplate for more comfortable use, and the twin compression springs and reversible heel plate carried over from the original late 1930s design. It was a market leader, as was the Supraphonic snare drum with its aluminium alloy (or, rarely, brass) shell, ten Imperial lugs and simple P83 snare strainer. Ludwig was also at the forefront in producing their own plastic heads - barely months behind Remo. All this put Ludwig in the strongest position to win over the rock drummers. Of course when Ringo Starr appeared as if from nowhere playing Ludwig (notably on the *Ed Sullivan* TV show in February 1964) the future was sealed. Ludwig would be number one for the next decade.

When The Beatles came to Chicago in 1964, Bill Ludwig Jnr took the opportunity to present Ringo with a 14-carat-gold-plated 5x14 Super-Sensitive snare drum which, in the ensuing crush, promptly disappeared. I've recently heard that Ringo does now have the drum. Is that correct, Ringo?

Of course Ringo wasn't Ludwig's only asset: they also had two very influential pre-rock endorsers. Buddy Rich had played WFL/Ludwig from the post-war years through to 1960, and from 1953 Ludwig had Joe Morello. Morello joined the Dave Brubeck Quartet in 1955 and scored a rare and massive jazz hit with 'Take Five'. The quartet's melodic, accessible jazz, with its European classical influence, quickly became popular with the college crowd. And Morello's immaculate technique and mastery of playing in 5/4 (or any other time signature thrown at him) made a profound impression on the young drummers who would later emerge in the progressive rock era. If jazz could mix time signatures like classical music, then so could rock. When Ludwig asked Morello to pick out a kit, instead of going for the expected white marine pearl – à la Buddy and Gene – Morello chose the unfashionable silver sparkle. Morello's silver sparkle Super Classic became the coolest kit of the 1960s along with Ringo's oyster black.

Ludwig were firmly established as *the* serious rock drums in both the US and Britain. They were seen with players of every style, from Dino Danelli and Johnny 'Bee' Badanjek (Mitch Ryder & The Detroit Wheels) through soul's Al Jackson to Spencer Dryden with Jefferson Airplane and John Densmore with The Doors. As heavy rock emerged, Ludwig appeared with Don Brewer of Grand Funk Railroad and Ian Paice of Deep Purple. In the 1970s John Bonham played Plexiglas Vista-lites and stainless steel Ludwigs, while Carmine Appice promoted the single-headed Octa-Plus melodic toms. Ludwig was the choice of most of rock's icons, including Nick Mason (Pink Floyd), Simon Kirke (Free), Roger Taylor (Queen), and thousands of others.

Ludwig addressed the move to louder playing with their beefed up Atlas hardware. However, in order to support the increasingly massive tom brackets, Ludwig changed their shell designs to six-ply straight-sided shells in the mid 1970s. They also stopped steam-bending and went to the modern method of using moulds. Although this was the direction most companies were taking, it still upset some of the traditional Ludwig fans.

As the decade turned Bill Ludwig Jnr took a decision which echoed his father's 1929 sale of Ludwig & Ludwig to Conn. In November of 1981 he sold Ludwig to Selmer. With the double threat posed by the Japanese expansion and the 1980s advent of electronic kits and drum machines, Ludwig had little option. Ludwig's days of innovation looked over. And yet Ludwig, more so than the other traditional American companies, still maintained a strong rock profile, with the likes of Alex van Halen, Joey Kramer of Aerosmith and Alan White of Yes. And the Gods smiled again in the late 1980s when Neil Peart picked out Ludwig in a *Modern Drummer* side-by-side comparison, resulting in a new generation of rockers checking out Ludwig for the first time.

It's somehow sad in the mid 1990s to see the Ludwig name on the budget Rocker series, with typically Taiwanese Pearl-clone hardware and fittings. But the Ludwig Classic/Super Classic look has not substantially changed other than with the introduction at the end of the 1980s of the (optional) full-length version of the Classic lug. The heavy Modular hardware is inevitable in the 1990s. The historic Imperial and Classic lugs have not been tampered with. Aluminium shells are still available at least on Acrolyte snare drums. The Classic (six-ply) and Super Classic (four-ply) are still made in the Ludwig maple/poplar mixes. In the mid 1990s it is again possible to buy a Black Beauty snare drum with a seamless brass shell, as opposed to the bronze shells which Ludwig maintained for many years were as good or better. And you can still buy a trusty Speedking bass drum pedal.

MAPEX

While following in the footsteps of the three major Japanese companies – Pearl, Tama and Yamaha – Mapex is very much a latecomer, having only been launched worldwide in 1989. Mapex is part of the KHS group which was founded in 1930, although the present Mapex drum factory in Taiwan has been operational since 1982. This factory has over the years produced drums for Sonor, Tama, Yamaha and Hohner. But it wasn't until 1991 that Mapex really got going when they took on Billy Cobham as their prime endorser and product adviser.

At first the Orion, Saturn and Mars kits were – surprise, surprise – not unlike a dozen other Pearl copies. And once Cobham came on board they started to look more like Tama. In the mid 1990s Mapex still hasn't achieved a unique identity. But they are now making professional drums comparable in quality with the opposition, and have impressive

96

endorsers including Mike Portnoy of Dream Theatre and Igor Cavalera of Brazilian HM growlers Sepultura.

Mapex's early Zero Contact resonance isolation system has been replaced by the niftier Isolated Tom System (ITS) introduced in 1993, and is even fitted to the budget line Mars Pro. The range has been expanded at both ends with the entry-level Venus series and the top professional Orion MapleTech. The MapleTech is offered with six-ply ⅓" maple shells with or without an outer veneer of Birdseye maple. Alternatively there's the Traditional MapleTech with thinner tom shells (⅛") and 24-carat gold-plated lugs.

BILL MATHER

Bill Mather was a Scottish drum shop owner in New York who in the late 1930s designed a shell-mount tom holder ('consolette'), spurs and cymbal stands, and marketed his ideas through Walberg & Auge. The consolette was used by top American companies right through to the 1970s.

MONTINERI

Joe Montineri was one of the first manufacturers of high quality rock-maple custom snare drums to embrace the retro 1920s solid brass tubular lug look. Montineri, based in the US, was also in the vanguard of 'soprano' snare sizes (4x12 and 5x12) and virtually unlimited custom finishes.

NOBLE & COOLEY

Noble & Cooley have a long and fascinating history. They made drums for the American Civil War, built a drum for Abraham Lincoln, no less, that was used in political rallies, and in 1876 made an 8" diameter drum for the American centennial celebrations. However, for most of their history Noble & Cooley have been making toy drums. In 1854 Silas Noble made 631 toy drums in his kitchen; within 20 years production had expanded to 100,000 toy and marching drums a year.

Today the company is run by John and Jay Jones, descendants of James P Cooley. Of most interest to us is the moment in 1976 when a local drummer, who had discovered that Noble & Cooley did steam bending, brought in a damaged Radio King to see if they could replace the shell. Jay Jones did this, and went on to do several more. In 1980 Noble & Cooley started experimenting with a solid-shell professional snare drum, and after four years released the Classic SS (Solid Shell) snare drum.

The shell was ¼" thick and made from New England green maple with ⁵⁄₁₆" maple reinforcing rings. The low mass brass tubular lugs would soon be seen on high-end snare drums from all the major manufacturers. Additionally, Noble & Cooley mounted each lug post at a single 'nodal point', the position of least interference with the shell's vibration. The strainer was also brass, while the rims were die-cast.

The new snare set a trend in the drum world for re-evaluating the designs and methods of the 1920s, and Noble & Cooley introduced a new generation to the pros and cons of solid versus ply shells, tubular lugs and die cast rims, the importance of snare beds, and so on.

Noble & Cooley followed with the Star maple series, an entire line of solid-shell drums. A cheaper line called Horizon has ply shells with all the plies arranged in the same direction, the idea being to emulate a solid-shell grain.

NOONAN

Gary Noonan is based in Kent, south-east England, where he renovates and customises drums. Since 1991 he's been making high quality snare drums and occasionally whole kits. Noonan snare drums are made in spun brass in different weights, while his wooden snares are made with stave (barrel) construction or cut from a solid block of mahogany.

NORTH

North drums were the original American fibreglass flared horn design, patented in 1971 by Roger North, an MIT engineering graduate. The drums were cylindrical, but bent through 90 degrees to project forwards. North claimed: "Our 'horn loaded' drums concentrate your sound and project it out to the audience." North also said that because of increased bass frequencies the toms could be of smaller diameter. The bass drums had a more normal shape, open at the front and slightly flared.

North started out in Portland, Oregon, and after some initial success production was moved to New York in 1977 and increased. Early users included Billy Cobham and Doug 'Cosmo' Clifford of Creedence Clearwater Revival. Gerry Brown had a flame painted five-piece North kit customised by Paul Jamieson who also helped Jeff Porcaro design his Pearl rack.

OLYMPIC

Olympic were the budget version of Premier drums, which helped many British rock stars to get started. The drums were actually of good quality, if a little more basic than Premier. The shells were the same but the hardware was more frugal, generally with six lugs on the bass drums and snare drums instead of eight, for example, and pressed steel rather than die-cast rims. The Olympic line was started back in 1937 but was going strong during the 1960s and lasted until the early 1980s. A line called Super Olympic was supplied to the US around the mid 1970s. Premier market an Olympic line today, but this is made in Taiwan rather than at the Premier factory.

ORANGE

see CAPELLE

PEARL

Pearl is today the world's largest drum manufacturer, with factories in Taiwan and the US, as well as the biggest drum factory in Japan. Pearl also has distribution companies in Nashville and North Hollywood, US, and in Milton Keynes, England. The company exclusively manufactures all its own parts, employs over 600 people worldwide, and exports to more than 55 countries.

The Pearl Instrument Co was founded in April 1946 when Katsumi Yanagisawa began manufacturing music stands, but in 1950 he started making drums and changed the name to Pearl Industries Ltd. By 1953 the Pearl Musical Instrument Company was producing a full line of percussion instruments for the Japanese market, and the following year Pearl began exporting to the US.

In 1957 Katsumi's eldest son, Mitsuo Yanagisawa, formed Pearl's worldwide export division with the motto: "Highest quality at lowest prices." In 1961 a large new factory was built at Chiba, Japan, to meet the expanding market for rock drum kits, and this is Pearl's current HQ. However, it was not until 1966 that Pearl produced a professional kit bearing its own name – the Pearl President.

Pearl continued to prosper and in 1968 a second drum factory was built near the first. But with the Japanese boom well under way and labour costs rising, in 1973 Pearl moved much of its production to Taiwan.

During the mid 1970s Pearl built drums with nine-ply wood shells, which when lined with fibreglass were called Image Creator. They also built concert toms in fibreglass only, a Plexiglas line called Crystallite, and a brass snare drum called the Jupiter. The tom mounts and bass drum pedal borrowed heavily from Rogers' Swiv-O-Matic designs. But Pearl already had flush fold-away spurs and the Rock-Lok toe-operated drop clutch for closing the hi-hat without using the hands. Here were clear intimations of Pearl's future hardware innovations.

By this time Pearl were turning heads with impressive endorsers including jazz legends Louie Bellson and Art Blakey as well as the great Nashville drummer Larrie Londin. By the early 1980s Pearl had Jeff Porcaro, Chester Thompson, Phil Collins, Jim Keltner and Ian Paice.

Porcaro was responsible for the introduction of the Pearl rack, made from square-section aluminium, which ushered in the modern era of rack systems. Other memorable Pearl innovations include the Free Floating Snare design, which allowed the interchange of different shells – wood, steel, brass and so on – within a single snare drum frame, while in the 1990s there is the Pearl Power Shifter bass drum pedals with quad faced beaters and extremely fine bearing action.

Pearl gradually developed a broader line than other manufacturers, including the Professional GLX (six-ply lacquered maple) and BLX (six-ply lacquered birch), and the budget Export. Pearl had previously catered for the cheap end of the market with the Maxwin brand; later, the Export took over and became the world's most successful drum kit by offering increasingly good value for money for the semi-pro drummer, and on a worldwide basis. A vast industry has developed in Taiwan churning out cheap copies of the Pearl Export

98

design. These kits are shipped all around the world and labelled with hundreds of different brandnames. The shells are made from red lauan (often called Philippine mahogany).

By the 1990s Pearl left behind the single square lug design and moved on to the fashionable flush-braced lug. This distinguished the Export from the myriad cheap clones. By the mid 1990s the Export Select had a birch inner liner to the shell, a natural wood lacquer finish, and a matching wood-shell 5x14 snare drum.

Pearl have come up with so many variations it's difficult to keep track, especially since each series is identified by dubiously related initials. For example in 1991 the CZX Custom series boasted heavy ten-ply maple shells with birdseye maple exteriors, while the SZX (CZX Studio) series had the same shell spec in birch. Then we had the (mid-priced) SLX (Prestige Session Elite) in seven-ply mahogany and birch, and the WLX (Prestige Session) Jazz with the same shells in matt finish. All very confusing.

It was a relief when Pearl, responding to 1990s trends, brought out their flagship Masters Custom series with the (ISS) Integrated Suspension System. The Masters Custom has four-ply ⅛" maple shells with four-ply reinforcing rings and small curved Gretsch-like lugs.

For their 50th anniversary in 1996 Pearl chose to produce a limited number of 1920s-style one-piece maple-shell snares with engraved flat-section rims, collar hooks, and tube lugs –

and all plated in 24-carat gold.

All Pearl one-piece maple shell snare drums are made from American maple in the Japanese plant. The maple board is softened in a microwave oven rather than by steam before bending around the mould. The shells are then cured for 30 days. It actually takes Pearl three months to make a drum, rather than the one day for an ordinary run-of-the-mill drum. Who says modern companies don't take care?

PEAVEY

Peavey is the well known Massachusetts-based manufacturer of amplifiers and electronic instruments. They first introduced conventional looking drums at the 1984 NAMM show, but these never made it into production. They then went back to the drawing board and came up with something startlingly different a decade later.

The main theory behind Peavey drums is the Radial Bridge System dreamed up by product development manager Steve Volpp. Volpp makes the analogy with an acoustic guitar: the drum head is equivalent to the strings, the shell is the soundboard and the 'radial' bridge is the bridge. On conventional drums the 'soundboard' (shell) is weighed down with lugs, bolts and so on. With the Peavey design the soundboard is one-tenth-of-an-inch-thick three-ply maple (bass drums are five-ply), is 'free floating' and can sustain fully. The stress is taken by the heavy wooden 'radial bridge' which incorporates the bearing edge and

supports the tension fittings. No mounting hardware touches the shells. The result is drums which are loud and open sounding – but they have an unusual look. The snare drum is the opposite of the toms with a massive wooden shell 1¾" thick and very heavy. This follows the usual principle that a thicker shell brings out the high overtones.

Peavey have extended their line to three different levels – the Radial Pro 500, 750 and 1000 – with a wide range of finishes including plastic pearls, coloured oils and glosses. Peavey's endorsers include Robin DiMaggio, Bobby Rock, and Pearson Grange (D-Ream).

PORK PIE PERCUSSION

Pork Pie Percussion in the US produce a line of Canadian hard-rock maple ply shells and solid maple snare drums with RIMS mounting. Pork Pie's Bill Detamore collaborated with Tama during the early 1990s in the design of Tama's Starclassic line.

PREMIER

The Premier Drum Company was founded in October 1922 by 20-year-old Albert Della-Porta, who with £27 capital (around $43) rented a basement in Berwick Street, central London.

Albert was a drummer who'd previously played Boyle drums and had ideas for improving them. When Charlie Boyle was killed in a fight in a London pub, effectively ending the Boyle drum company, Della-Porta took on Boyle's production manager George Smith and began making drums. They were soon joined by Albert's younger brother Fred, a sax player, and in 1924, on moving to larger premises in Berwick Street, Fred became Sales Director.

Until 1925 Premier made drums for others to label. But when their biggest customer, John E Dallas, requested seasonal discounts, Premier decided from that point they would only make drums bearing their own name. During the 1920s and 1930s production moved to south London and then to Park Royal on the western outskirts of the city, and a showroom was established in Golden Square in central London (where today Foote's drum store remains as Premier's London showcase).

By the early 1930s Premier was a major manufacturer of consoles, exporting to the US. During World War II Premier was engaged in making sights for anti-tank guns, among other things, and the accuracy of the company's manufacturing increased dramatically. The Park Royal factory was burnt down during an air raid in September 1940, and the Ministry of Supply relocated Premier to Wigston, just outside Leicester in central England. After the war, Premier invested in die-casting machinery and quickly re-established their supremacy in the home market.

George Smith retired in 1956. Fred della Porta continued to build Premier's vast overseas trade, up to his retirement in 1972 (after which he remained chairman of Foote's). Albert della Porta died in 1965 and his three

sons took over the reins: Clifford as Chairman, Gerald as Managing Director and Raymond as Production Director.

Clifford had joined the company in the late 1940s and as a drummer with an engineering degree he headed the dynamic design and research department. Premier were well known for their flush based stands which were sturdier than most others, thanks to exclusively die-cast components. Premier also made die-cast rims from mazac (the same alloy as used by Gretsch) and flush–braced lugs plated in 'diamond' chrome, a three-stage process with layers of copper, nickel and chromium individually polished. In 1958, barely months after Remo, Premier introduced Everplay plastic heads, made from ICI's Melinex. Premier at this time made Krut, Zyn and Super Zyn cymbals too. Cymbal making eventually stopped, but to this day Premier make a complete range of excellent quality heads.

Premier were unassailable in the domestic market and by 1968 were exporting to 104 countries. The brand had been a favourite of American jazz legends right from the days of Chick Webb in the 1930s, followed by Louis Armstrong's Barrett Deems (known as the fastest drummer in the world). During the 1950s and 1960s Premier were the choice of Kenny Clarke, Gus Johnson (Ella Fitzgerald), Philly Jo Jones, Sam Woodyard (Duke Ellington), Rashied Ali (John Coltrane), Bill 'Beaver' Harris (Archie Shepp), Max Roach, Louis Hayes (Cannonball Adderley, Oscar

Peterson) and many others.

The Premier Royal Ace snare drum was played by virtually every British drummer at some time during the 1950s and 1960s. It had eight flush lugs, die-cast hoops and was available in depths from 4" to 12", the 5½" wood-shell drum being the most common. The Royal Aces featured full shell-width snares operated by an internal double-bar mechanism described as a "floating parallel action". The chunky pull-away lever action was always rather stiff. The simpler Hi Fi snare range with side-action throw-off was probably more efficient. The Royal Ace evolved into the 2000 line with 'Flobeam', the summit of the parallel design. Premier also made in the late 1970s the 35, a centre–beaded aluminium-shell snare with ten lugs that was a belated response to Ludwig's market-leading 400 model.

When Ringo Starr first appeared with The Beatles he was playing Premier, as were most other British rockers. But as soon as success was in the air he changed to Ludwig, opening the floodgates to American kits. With the complete reversal of British pop musicians' fortunes – from village hall no-hopers to American idols almost overnight – the previously unattainable American gear was now a must-have. But as all things British became trendy during the 1960s, Premier's overseas sales continued to prosper. Around 1977 Premier moved to their large purpose built factory at Blaby Road in Wigston, not far from the old site.

Premier continued to produce

good kits in the 1970s and 1980s, in particular the Resonator with its inner two-ply lining forming a separate sound chamber within the shell. The Resonator featured two of Premier's trademarks, the die-cast rims and flush bracing. But Premier also made concessions to fashion, and the Projector series featured single-ended lugs and triple-flange rims. Premier had even finally produced a 9x13 tom to replace their oddball 8x14, and in the mid 1970s started to phase in Trilok tripod-base stands.

Having survived a mauling by the Americans in the 1960s and 1970s, Premier were unable to keep up with the Japanese. The oriental companies revolutionised hardware design and shell making, putting Premier in trouble (along with the Americans). In October 1983 Premier's board of directors resigned and Premier went into the hands of the Official Receiver. However the 11-strong management team formed a consortium to buy the company as a going concern, and in April 1984 the company was restarted as Premier Percussion. The team struggled on until the banks appointed Tony Doughty as Executive Chairman. Doughty managed to negotiate a merger with Yamaha in October 1987. Yamaha brought in much needed capital and modernised Premier to the point that when Yamaha left in 1992, Premier was totally rejuvenated.

Premier launched probably their best drum series ever, the Signia, in 1992. The Signia takes Premier's philosophy of the thin shell with reinforcing rings – but for

the first time for Premier the drums are made from maple rather than birch. This was followed in 1994 by the Genista, this time using traditional Finnish birch but with a straight-walled shell. Premier's budget APK (Advanced Power Kit) and the XPK with lacquered birch finish have continued to keep pace with the market leading Pearl Export.

PURECUSSION

PureCussion is the American company which produces the RIMS Resonance Isolation Mounting System designed by Gary Gauger. Gauger first started to experiment with resonance mounting in 1972, and the session drummer Russ Kunkel (James Taylor) tried out the prototypes. This led to the start of Gauger Percussion, and as business expanded Gauger entered into a licensing agreement with Robert Carlson of the Quadion Corporation of Minneapolis to produce RIMS. They then set up the PureCussion company, in December 1984.

RIMS mounts have been used by numerous drummers on almost every make of drum. During the 1990s the major drum manufacturers have devised their own mounts with similar function, or supplied RIMS mounts under license. RIMS mounts in chrome or black finish are available for mounted toms (R), floor toms (FT), snare drums (S) and mounted floor toms (RM). PureCussion also produces easily transportable shell-less drum kits, and have recently started to make maple drums with 'Tour Tuff' finishes.

REMO

Up to a decade ago Remo Belli was best known as the name on the world's most popular drum heads. However, since the mid 1980s Remo has also become a successful manufacturer of drum kits, and during the 1990s the company has added a colourful line of world percussion. The shells for the drum kits and for the various items of percussion are all made from a synthetic material called Acousticon. This is made from crushed wood fibres, pulped in similar fashion to paper and then tightly rolled in continuous laminations to the required thickness. The resulting shell is hardened by heating and impregnating with silica resins. One advantage of this process is that any size and thickness of shell is possible, and any shape – hence the suitability of Acousticon for sculpting congas, djemes and so on. Remo has continued to improve the formulation of Acousticon to its present 'R' designation.

Actually Remo had scored a hit in the 1970s with their shell-less Roto-toms which showed that the drum head generates most of the sound without any need for a shell. (Roto-toms were actually conceived by Al Payson, percussionist with the Chicago Symphony Orchestra in 1968.) Remo manufactured Roto-toms in a wide range of sizes, from 6" to 18" diameter, and these could instantly be tuned to different pitches by rotating the cast metal frame. For this reason the larger Roto-toms were also used as cheap substitutes for timpani. Roto-tom frames (without the heads) were in 1988 adapted by Remo's Rick Drumm to be played in a bell-like or hi-hat-like fashion. Top Remo endorser Terry Bozzio made brilliant use of them.

In the early 1980s Remo went beyond the Roto-tom concept to produce PTS Pre-tuned heads. These heads were tensioned on their own hoop and could simply be clipped onto PTS kits (1982) without any further tensioning. Although the PTS idea had limited success it marked the start of Remo's kit making, which was the path the company subsequently followed. The first proper kit was called the Encore and appeared in the mid 1980s. Liberator and Innovator PTS kits were marketed in the late 1980s alongside Encore and Discovery conventionally tuned lines. Then there was the easily-transportable, single-headed Legero. The top-of-the-line Mastertouch was introduced in 1988.

Remo produced their own lines of hardware and the kits were covered in a coloured plastic material called Quadura. In the mid 1990s Mastertouch kits are available with a real maple veneer applied to the Quadura and called VenWood.

ROGERS (American)

The Rogers company dates back to 1849 and Joseph Rogers, an Irish emigrant from Dublin who came to America and produced drum and banjo heads. Rogers didn't start to market drums until the middle of the 1930s, when they were located in Farmingdale, New Jersey. Even

then the actual drums and hardware were bought in from other manufacturers, but were fitted with Rogers' skins which, according to Bill Ludwig Jnr, were highly regarded.

Joseph Rogers' grandson, Cleveland Rogers, had no children and so he sold the company to one Henry Grossman in 1953, and the business was moved to Covington, Ohio. Grossman had a couple of employees who were to play a major part in transforming Rogers from also-rans to the cutting edge of American drum design over the next decade.

Joe Thompson was the brilliant design engineer and Ben Strauss the marketing brain behind the Rogers revolution. Thompson set about redesigning all the Rogers fittings and hardware, and the Rogers Swiv-O-Matic system hardware which first appeared in 1957 set the pace for many years.

The Swiv-O-Matic tom holder finally displaced Bill Mather's ubiquitous consolette holder, and the Swiv-O-Matic hi-hat and bass drum pedals were equally popular. The bass drum pedal could be attached at an angle and the height of the footboard altered. The Swiv-O-Matic concept was based on an egg shaped ball joined to high grade steel shafts which were made of hexagonal ('hex') section to prevent turning and slipping. The ball was tightened down into its socket using a drum key. Additionally there were the 'Knobby' fittings: a telescopic cymbal holder, and floor tom legs (the first to be bent for stability).

By the early 1960s the most

obvious remaining weakness in the Rogers design was the oblong lugs which were prone to hairline cracks. They were finally replaced by the so-called 'Beavertail' scalloped lugs from 1964. From then until late into the 1970s Rogers drums, with their Keller five-ply maple shells, were arguably the best American drums.

Also revolutionary was Rogers' ten-lug Dyna-Sonic snare drum which had a chromed brass shell made stronger by the extra flanges cunningly incorporated in the bearing edges. The Dyna-Sonic had snares carried in a cast aluminium frame suspended beneath the drum. When the snares were engaged they were lifted up against the bottom head, rather than strained against it which tends to choke the head. Thus the drum had increased sensitivity and projection.

The budget snare drum was the eight-lug PowerTone which had a straightforward side lever throw-off. It was also available in 5" and 6½" depths with a chromed brass or maple shell. The strangest snare drum Rogers made was the Skinny 2½x13, also known as the Satellite. The top and bottom triple-flanged rims screwed directly into the central grey cast block.

In 1966 Rogers was purchased by CBS. Manufacturing remained in Covington, but the offices and warehouses moved to Dayton, Ohio, while in 1969 CBS moved the entire operation to Fullerton in California.

Rogers continued to be innovative. In the mid 1970s the company introduced MemriLoc hardware, which employed 1"-

diameter tubing in place of the hexagonal rods. Crucially, in order to prevent slipping, the tubing had extra MemriLoc clamps at each joint, adjustable with a drum key. This simple idea had the additional virtue of ensuring you could duplicate your exact set-up every time. Memory locks are of course today included in every manufacturer's hardware. Nonetheless this was Rogers' swansong. By the start of the 1980s Rogers had been reduced to a shadow of its former glory by the Japanese onslaught.

ROGERS (British)

At the time of the British rock invasion Rogers were the most expensive American drums. Ludwig were more than 50 per cent more costly in Britain than Premier and beyond the means of all but the professionals. Rogers prices would also have been prohibitive, so for a few years in the early to mid 1960s Rogers sent hardware to north London where Boosey & Hawkes transformed their Ajax shells into Rogers drums. In due course copies were made of the Rogers hardware, but due to variations in local materials the fittings are not compatible with the American originals.

Rogers fared quite well in Britain, and Dave Clark inspired early interest with his distinctive five-piece kit which was known right through the 1970s as the Londoner V. The standard four-piece was called the Starlighter. As the fashion for larger kits progressed, Rogers offered the Greater Londoner VIII, Custom

Londoner IX, and the Studio kits which included concert toms. The DynaSonic chrome-over-brass snare was still included but now with the extended-height Supreme hi-hat (with silent centre-pull action) and the Supreme bass pedal (with industrial belting strap and broader footplate).

ROSE-MORRIS

The story of the Rose-Morris connection with drums can be taken right back to 1832 and a London firm of pen-nib makers called Henry Solomon & Co. About 30 years later they became Barnet Samuel, and moved into musical instrument making (as well as coining the tradename Decca for a portable record player in 1914). Around 1905, Barnet Samuel had come up with an English-sounding name, John Grey & Sons, for imported and home-made banjos, drums and other instruments. In 1932 Barnet Samuel were bought out by the Rose-Morris company which carried on manufacturing drums under the names John Grey, Autocrat, Broadway and Shaftesbury, as well as Clansman military drums.

In the mid 1960s the Autocrat range had double-headed tom toms, eight-lug snare drums, bass drums and floor toms, and a five-lug small tom. Bass drum depths were quoted as 17" and 15". (Autocrat, Premier and others at the time included the wooden hoops in these measurements; today they would be called 14" and 12" drums.) The Supreme kit had four drums and three (Premier) Super Zyn cymbals, while

the Modern outfit had three drums and three Zyns.

John Grey Broadway drums were the budget versions of the Autocrats, with six lugs on the snare and bass (eight on the floor) and single- or double-headed toms. The four-drum kit was called the Super.

In the late 1960s Rose-Morris marketed kits under their own brandname, RM. The kit still had die-cast Premier-style rims, flush-base stands, a new 'flame' finish, a ball-and-socket tom holder, fold-out spurs, "sleek new tension fittings" (lugs which look suspiciously like the old Autocrats), and a direct centre-pull hi-hat with flush base. The finishes were pretty snazzy, including Crystal, Ruby, Sapphire Flame, Opal Flame, Champagne Glitter, Red Glitter, and so on. Rose-Morris also produced Headmaster plastic heads.

In the mid 1970s Rose-Morris was still marketing drums, including the Shaftesbury line of acrylic Vistalite copies.

EDDIE RYAN

During the 1970s and 1980s Eddie Ryan custom made drums and kits with distinctive square nut boxes and red and blue shields. Customers of the British maker included Neil Conti of Prefab Sprout, Dave Mattacks, and Pick Withers (the original Dire Straits drummer). Ryan took over the premises in Archer Street, central London, where the legendary Len 'Doc' Hunt had his workshops and hire business. Archer Street had been the location where British jazz

103

and dance band musicians would gather every Monday to swap gigs and gossip in the days before every house had a telephone.

SLEISHMAN

Don Sleishman is a drummer from Sydney, Australia, who custom builds drums using his patented Suspended Shell system. The shell is totally free of any fittings and is held in place only by the heads. This goes one step further than Pearl's Free Floating System and Peavey's recent Radial Bridge system. Sleishman's solution involves a solid steel-ring frame to which the tension rods are fastened; by removing the batter head the shell simply lifts out. The shells are Keller-made Canadian rock-maple, but options include block construction snares (similar to Brady) in jarrah and padauk. Needless to say these are not cheap. Another option is an extremely dense fibreglass shell. The Suspended Shell is just one of Sleishman's clever inventions – he also produced a beautifully engineered double bass drum pedal way back in 1965.

SLINGERLAND

Henry H Slingerland started his company in Chicago in 1916, selling May Bell and Slingerland banjos from the 1920s and following with drums around 1927. As with their main rivals Ludwig & Ludwig and Leedy, Slingerland made brass snare drums in the popular Black Beauty engraved finish or used solid walnut, maple and mahogany.

As the prime up-and-coming company, Slingerland lent a sympathetic ear to Gene Krupa's requests for a revolutionary drum kit with tuneable bottom heads on the tom toms. Slingerland obviously made the right decision because Krupa went on to become a huge star and the Radio King drums set the pace for years to come. Krupa also evidently made the right decision since the Radio King snare drums are to this day regarded by some drummers as the best snare drums ever made. However, the tom toms and bass drums in three-ply mahogany are generally not so highly regarded.

Krupa's fame spread from his first appearance with the Benny Goodman orchestra in the mid 1930s. The band became the major live attraction right across the US and Krupa's tom tom assaults on Goodman's 1937 recording of 'Sing Sing Sing' led to the drum solo becoming an expected highlight of swing-era concerts, making stars of many big band drummers in the process. Virtually overnight, the vaudeville kit with consoles and Chinese toms and effects was stripped down to the four-piece modern drum kit.

Slingerland persisted with solid-shell Radio King snare drums long after other companies had stopped producing this type of drum. Although the Radio King is today seen as the standard for solid-shell snare drums, probably more important was the Radio king kit's introduction of the modern tuneable double-headed tom tom. By the late 1930s Radio King toms were available in a very respectable range from 8" to 16", and they

featured cast Streamlined lugs with swivel nuts to ease alignment and prevent thread stripping.

Radio King kits were very successful right through to the mid 1950s, but by the rock era of the 1960s Slingerland were trailing behind Ludwig and Gretsch. Leedy had been bought by Slingerland – and was never developed. Ludwig had survived its trials and became the big success story of the rock era. Ironically, Slingerland were by then making probably their best drum kits. Around the middle 1950s they had belatedly moved to triple-flanged 'Rim Shot' rims, and had introduced the modern, rounded Sound King lug.

Throughout the 1970s Slingerland made excellent drums with quality maple shells (three-ply with reinforcing hoops; five-ply without). The Zoomatic snare strainer was an improvement on earlier models as was the Set-o-matic tom holder which by rotating through 180 degrees could be adapted to left-handed or right-handed set-ups. Variety was also offered by means of concert tom kits and Cut-A-Way toms derived from Slingerland's marching band division. Then there was the Spitfire snare drum with 12 double-ended lugs, and the Two-To-One with 12 lugs on top and six below. Both were available with wood or chrome-over-brass shells, and with combination gut-and-wire snares. There was also the Artist maple-shell and Student aluminium-shell snare drums.

Slingerland's hardware included memorable items such as the Yellow Jacket twin-spring bass drum pedal and the sturdy

Dynamo hi-hat. Around the 1980s came the Magnum Force hardware which showed Slingerland was still trying to keep up with the expanding rock world – and indeed many rock players have played Slingerland, including Nigel Olssen with Elton John and Bev Bevan of ELO. But like Gretsch and Rogers, Slingerland still trailed behind Ludwig, never quite capturing the big name rock endorsers to elevate their profile, even if they did have jazz greats Louie Bellson and Buddy Rich... and Neil Peart in his early days.

As the 1980s progressed Slingerland, like the other American companies, dropped further out of the scene. They were bought by Gretsch who, presumably, had enough problems of their own and did little for Slingerland. Inevitably a budget series appeared, the Slingerland Spirit 1000 and 2000 with Taiwanese 'mahogany' shells. A 'Lite' top-of-the-line kit was announced in 1990; it was American-made with ¼" five-ply maple shell toms, and ⅓" six-ply snare and bass drums, all finished in high-gloss lacquer and fitted with Evans heads.

In the 1990s Radio King snare drums are still on offer with single-ply, steam bent 5½" and 6½" maple shells. Slingerland claim, curiously, that the Radio King "produces its distinctive sound due to a fortunate manufacturing imperfection – the heads fit too tightly on the shell, interfering with their vibrations and giving rise to the ringy Radio King sound, with low sustain and characteristic overtones."

In the mid 1990s Slingerland has been taken over by the Gibson company and are now producing the Studio King line in Nashville. The drums feature straight-sided maple shells with six-ply toms up to 16" and eight-ply bass drums and 18" floor toms. The snare drum is a ten-ply. The drums are a continuation of Slingerland's classic look with familiar lugs and Stick Saver die-cast rims, and Slingerland 'cloud' badges in bronze. Kits are supplied with 5000-series hardware and RIMS mounts. Gregg Bissonette has recently been playing a beautifully customised Slingerland Studio King kit in Green Maple Frost finish, and Taylor Hawkins with Alanis Morissette has a red glitter Slingerland.

SONOR

Sonor is the leading European drum manufacturer along with Premier. Sonor has been producing quality drums throughout the present century. It was most likely a brass-shelled Sonor snare drum which inspired William Ludwig Snr to produce the first Ludwig & Ludwig metal shell snare drums early in the 20th century.

Sonor was founded in Bavaria, southern Germany, in 1875 by Johannes Link. Link began by making military drums but by the turn of the century he had over 50 employees making timpani, concert percussion and cymbals. By the early 1920s, with three times as many workers, Link started to make complete drum kits.

The business survived the traumatic events of Germany's modern history under Johannes' son Otto and, later, Otto's son Horst. But in 1950 the Sonor factory was expropriated by the East German government and Sonor moved to West Germany, effectively starting over. When Otto Link died in 1955 the company was rebuilding itself steadily.

Sonor drums were distributed by Hohner in Britain and the USA during the 1960s, but in the UK they were overshadowed by the more striking Trixon drums. A Melody Maker ad from 1966, for example, offered the Sonor Chicago Star kit in red stripe at 145gns (£152.25, or about $245). It took until the end of the 1970s before Sonor were sufficiently confident to advertise themselves as the 'Rolls Royce' of drums, a claim which was borne out with the launch of the Signature series in 1980. With its mighty 12-ply beech shells and colossal hardware it finally established Sonor as a major company with a reputation for the finest workmanship and quality. The company continued in family ownership until 1991 when it was sold to the Hohner corporation.

For all its quality the thick (½") shell Signature soon looked out of step with 1980s thinking. Sonor therefore produced the ¼" shell birch Sonorlite in the mid 1980s. This was followed by the HiLite and HiLite Exclusive (1988), Sonor's first all-maple drums with nine-ply shells. The HiLite was also the first modern Sonor kit to feature retro tubular pipe lugs and rubber insulators.

By now Sonor was firmly

associated with top quality lines, but in the mid 1980s they produced a mid-price line, the Performer. This was replaced in 1990 by the Force 2000, with tubular lugs and nine-ply poplar shells, followed a year later by the Force 3000, with nine- and 11-ply birch shells, and finally the budget Force 1000 of 1992. The Force Maple appeared in the mid 1990s followed by the Sonic Plus with 6 and 9 ply birch shells.

Meanwhile, in 1991 the Signature had been updated to the Special Edition, and now in the mid 1990s Sonor has excelled itself once more with the Designer series, their most luxurious series yet.

Sonor artists include the session giant Bernard Purdie, Chester Thompson (Genesis), top clinician Steve Smith (Journey, Stuff, Vital Information) and Britain's Richard Bailey (Jeff Beck, Incognito, Billy Ocean).

STACCATO

Staccato appeared in 1977 and carried on to around 1984. They were amazing looking fibreglass drums designed by Pat Townsend, who says the idea came from a tree he once painted. The bass drum flares out in a double 'trouser leg' shape, the first asymmetrical drum ever patented. They were fitted with Hayman circular lugs and were the British equivalent of North drums, although North had a simpler 'alpine horn' shape.

The drums were loud and eye-catching and many of the great names of British rock – including Keith Moon, Mitch Mitchell, John Bonham and Simon Phillips – gave them a work out. The visual aspect of Staccato has appealed to many, including Malcolm McLaren's punk band Bow Wow Wow, who featured them on TV.

Unfortunately the history of Staccato is as convoluted as the drums, involving various names on the British drum scene. Drummer Chris Slade (who started out with Tom Jones and went on to Manfred Mann's Earthband and Uriah Heep) manufactured them in the early 1980s; Nicko McBrain was involved at one stage; and Pat Townsend recently said he was going to manufacture new Staccato drums using lighter carbon fibre. In recent years Staccato have been produced by the Canadian company Ayotte.

STRATFORD

Stratford drums were common in early-1960s Britain and were part of the Boosey & Hawkes/Ajax stable. Although Stratford and Edgware drums were marketed as cheaper lines than Ajax they ended up as more or less the same drums. Snares had the sharp bullet single tension lugs, offset slightly from one another vertically since they overlapped in length.

TAMA

The Hoshino family of Nagoya, Japan, started to sell musical instruments from their bookstore in 1908, later importing Ludwig and Slingerland drums from the US. Beginning in the mid 1950s they exported drums with the brandname Star ('hoshi' in Japanese means star). From 1962 their factory in Nagoya made musical instruments and later exported Hoshino Star drums.

It was not until after 1974 that the Tama name was used on drums. Tama concentrated at first on hardware, which was appropriate at that time of rock expansion. The Titan range included the first production boom cymbal stand and set the pace for rock-solid hardware with double-braced 36" spread tripods and chunky rubber feet.

Tama's design engineer Naohiro Yasuda came up with another couple of brilliantly simple ideas: nylon constriction-bushings in the telescopic joints; and the Multi-Clamp which allowed drummers to add on extra cymbal arms, cowbells and so on wherever they wanted. These ideas have been taken up by all the other companies. Tama also developed its own memory-lock system, called Key Lock, and added Touchlock one-touch securing levers for height adjustment in the mid 1980s.

Initially Tama's most important star adviser was Billy Cobham who helped them design their first top line kit in December 1977, the Superstar with lacquered shells of six-ply birch. Cobham's kit also featured the gong drum, a single-headed stand-mounted bass drum with oversize head. Tama was quickly establishing a strong identity, and this was further helped by Octobans, two sets of four 6"-diameter fibreglass tubes of differing lengths producing a clearly tuneable octave range. They were memorably used by Stewart Copeland alongside his Imperial Star kit, while today Simon Phillips cleverly weaves them into his intricate funk fusion patterns lending them a more melodic slant.

Tama gradually phased out the Superstar series and replaced it with the Artstar I (1983) and Artstar II (1986), made from nine-ply Canadian hard rock maple, complemented by the Granstar with eight-ply Japanese birch shells. Also during this period Tama developed a wide variety of snare drums, starting with the Mastercraft in bell brass, 12-ply rosewood, fibreglass, six-ply maple, and expanding to include birch, solid maple, birdseye maple, not to mention copper, brass, bell brass and steel. All of this was certainly impressive – and Tama even offered options in snare wire: steel aircraft control cable, or bell brass. The company also continued to innovate with hardware ideas, including the inwardly leaning Titan Stilt stands.

Not surprisingly, Tama attracted a who's-who of the rock world including the major role models Neil Peart and Lars Ulrich. After all this activity Tama inevitably had a quiet period as the 1990s dawned. They introduced the impressive Iron Cobra bass drum pedal range in 1993, but what they were really working on was the Starclassic drums. A change was in the air with the industry's wholesale move to vintage concepts of drum making and Tama, as they later claimed, had "gone back to basics". The Starclassic in maple or birch with nine-ply ⅓" thin shells

and low mass fittings shows that Tama has a lot yet to offer.

TRIXON

Trixon drums are regarded with nostalgic reverence by many, not least because they were without doubt the weirdest kits of the 1960s. Karl-Heinz Weimer's company, based in the seaport of Hamburg, northern Germany, was nothing if not experimental. Sometimes Trixon was innovative, but many of the ideas were novelties – and if they worked, that was a bonus.

Hamburg was devastated during World War II. It was rebuilt during the 1950s and returned the favour with two major gifts. First was The Beatles, who learned their craft here, and second was the enterprising and inventive Karl-Heinz Weimer who made Trixon instruments unique in the history of the drum kit.

Three main outfits were available by the early 1960s. The standard kit used by most drummers was the Luxus, but the sizes were sometimes rather eccentric: I've seen listings quoting 15 x 22 or 16 x 20 bass drums, alongside 14x24, as well as 8 x14, 4½x14, 6 x14, 5 x14, 3 x14 and 3 x13 snares, 9 x13 mounted tom and 17x18 floor tom. The earlier three-ply shells with reinforcing rings were later changed to six-ply, probably birch, or sometimes beech.

The Speedfire (0/700 series) was probably the most unusual kit. The bass drum had a squashed egg shape, described by Trixon as "two differently sounding bass

drums in one". Two bass pedals could be mounted along the batter hoop, though how you were supposed to play them is a mystery. The kit included up to five single-headed toms running the 'wrong' way on a special console–like rack.

The Telstar (Model 2000) had conical shells, as follows: 20" bass drum batter with wooden hoop, to 16" front with metal rim; 16" floor tom batter, to 20" bottom with metal rim; 13" mounted tom batter, and 12" bottom; 14" snare batter, and 13" bottom. The novelty value of the Telstar appealed to many, including Britain's Gerry & The Pacemakers who followed The Beatles down to London from Liverpool. Freddy Marsden, Gerry's brother who played drums in the band, was often seen with his red Croco finish Telstar.

Trixon finishes were, as you might expect, equally a mixture of the normal and the weird: plain black; blue, red, gold, green or silver glitter; blue, red, silver or gold Croco; red, grey, white marine, blue stripe, red stripe, grey stripe or white stripe pearls. The Telstar was primarily available only in Croco, which was reminiscent of those slides of oil that were projected at 1960s drop-out happenings.

Trixon had some ingenious hardware ideas, too. They had 'Shipform'-socket cast brackets (in the plan shape of a ship's hull) with central holes through which passed the tom mount tubes, bass drum spurs and so on. As a measure of Trixon's vision, the idea of a disappearing tom mount penetrating both bass drum and tom tom is the basis of the world beating Pearl-type mount, ubiquitous throughout the 1980s, while Trixon's disappearing cymbal mount, which had the rod passing through a clamped ball, was resurrected by the Sonor Designer hardware in the mid 1990s.

Trixon were also available in the US, branded either as Trixon or Vox. They were played by jazz vibes players Lionel Hampton and Victor Feldman (Trixon also made quality vibraphones) and by Sam Woodyard with Duke Ellington. A 1965 American pricelist shows the Luxus at $490, Speedfire at $525 and Telstar $515. In 1967 Weimer adapted the Luxus to suit Buddy Rich and added a metal-shell snare drum with parallel action, adjustable at both ends. Buddy played the kit from the beginning to the middle of 1967 (after which he briefly tried Fibes and then went on to Slingerland for the next decade).

Trixon did set up a manufacturing plant in Shannon in Ireland in the late 1960s, but despite Rich's late endorsement the company lost out to the Ludwig's invasion of Europe, and had disappeared by the early 1970s.

WALBERG & AUGE

From 1905 through to the 1960s Walburg & Auge of Worcester, Massachusetts, manufactured hardware for all the major American drum companies. In particular, Barney Walberg has been credited with producing the first hi-hat around 1926, which he did by experimentally extending the vertical tube of a 'low-boy'. Walberg & Auge also cornered the market in tom brackets for decades. Starting from the rail console design in the late 1930s, independent designer Bill Mather produced a much reduced consolette which bolted to the top of the bass drum and, by means of a hinged bracket, was slotted into a diamond-shaped plate screwed into the small tom. This design was supplied by Walberg & Auge right up to the late 1960s when the rock explosion necessitated stronger and more flexible mounts. The company's Buck Rogers snare drum stand was another item which appeared in the catalogues of many manufacturers, the name being taken from the fictional space character and nothing to do with the Rogers drum company. Walberg & Auge finally disappeared in 1979.

GEORGE WAY

The George Way Drum Company existed briefly from 1955 until 1961 when it was taken over by Camco. Way decided to branch out under his own name when CG Conn closed down the Leedy and Ludwig drum division in 1955. Way managed to raise the finance to lease the old Leedy factory – the Buescher Building – in Elkhart, Indiana, and sold his own line of George Way drums from 1957. They had a very modern appearance with the distinctive turret lug – at one time called the Aristocrat – which now adorns DW drums by way of Camco. As with Ulysses Leedy, the name George Way may not mean much to the average rock drummer today, but his influence on the development of drums in the first half of the 20th century through innovations such as the die-cast lug with swivel nut is immense.

YAMAHA

Yamaha is today a vast corporation with a bewilderingly diverse list of interests, from motorcycles to tennis rackets, so it's reassuring to know that Yamaha began when Torakusu Yamaha made the first Yamaha organ in 1887. Two years later he set up the Yamaha Organ Manufacturing Company in Hamamatsu, Japan. The name was changed to Nippon Gakki Co Ltd in 1897, and in 1900 the first Yamaha upright pianos were produced. In 1987 – the company's centennial year – the name was changed to the Yamaha Corporation. Today Yamaha is the largest musical instrument manufacturer in the world.

It was not until 1968 that the first Yamaha drums were produced in the Shinzu factory in Hamamatsu. The early drums looked like the Ludwig Super Classic with oyster pearl finish and consolette tom mount. But as with Tama and Pearl it didn't take too long before Yamaha leap-frogged into the top bracket. In 1975 Yamaha launched the 9000 Recording Custom series, designed by Takashi Hagiwara ('Hagi'). It featured six-ply straight walled birch shells with 45-degree bearing edges. The drums popularised two features in particular which became industry standards throughout the 1980s: hi-tension flush-braced lugs; and 'piano' lacquered shells.

The shells were superbly constructed using Yamaha's patented staggered-joint Air Seal System and flawlessly finished inside and out. The hardware was also brilliantly designed, and was relatively lightweight after a decade in which everything had got heavier and heavier. A distinctive feature was the use of a floor stand in place of traditional legs to support the large toms. The tom brackets have a 1"-diameter resinated ball clamp and hexagonal steel rods reminiscent of but improving upon Rogers' Swiv-O-Matic.

While the 9000 defined the studio and fusion sound of the 1980s, Yamaha were perhaps not so strong in the rock market. In the early 1980s Yamaha had the 7000 series with birch/lauan shells and arrow shaped lugs; this graduated to the Tour series in the mid 1980s and, around 1990, the Rock Tour Custom (RTC). Aside from the badge and finishes this looked exactly like the flush-braced 9000, but the shells were eight-ply (toms) and 11-ply (bass drums) in combined birch and lauan.

The budget end of Yamaha's range was also a slow starter. The 5000 series of the early 1980s eventually became the Power V, and in the mid 1990s we have the Stage Custom. Again, this is cosmetically similar to the 9000 and is the closest Yamaha have come to the Pearl Export market.

It seems Yamaha's best bet has always been in the high end market, and to prove this in 1991

Yamaha produced a totally new series, the Maple Customs. Again designed by Hagiwara, it features seven-ply toms and ten-ply bass drums with a completely different low mass button-type lug.

In 1993 Yamaha introduced its Yamaha Enhanced Sustain System (YESS) mounting hardware. This is now standard on the Maple Customs, and for its 20th anniversary in 1995 the RC-9000 too was revamped with YESS mounting brackets. It still looks a great kit.

The brighter, open sound of the Maple Customs may attract more rock players to Yamaha. Not that Yamaha has been short on rock endorsers – such as Larry Mullen (U2), Mickey Curry (Bryan Adams) and Mike Bordin (Faith No More) – but they've been slightly overshadowed by Yamaha's strong roster of fusion artists, starting with the ace, Steve Gadd, and following with Vinnie Colaiuta, Dave Weckl, Peter Erskine and David Garibaldi. These meticulous players have all been awarded with their own individual snare drum models in the 1990s: Weckl's with dual snares, Garibaldi's an aluminium piccolo, Erskine's paired 4x10 and 4x12 models, and Gadd with a range of no less than six.

ZICKOS

Zickos were reputedly the world's first commercially produced clear acrylic drums, made during the 1960s up to the early 1970s. Founder William Zickos, based in Kansas, is reported to be producing the drums again in 1996.

Page numbers in **bold** refer to illustrations.
Page numbers in *italics* refer to a company entry in the Drum Directory.
Band names as well as artists are included, in an effort to help some of those who-played-with-which-band arguments.

110

113

OWNERS' CREDITS

Drums photographed came from the following individuals' and organisations' collections, and we are most grateful for their help.

The owners are listed here in the alphabetical order of the code used to identify their instruments in the Key To Drum Photographs below.

AB Sir Alan Buckley (Classic Drum Museum); **AR** Arbiter Group; **BB** Brian Bennett; **BE** Beat About The Bush; **BL** Brian Lewis (Classic Drum Museum); **CC** Clem Cattini; **CK** Cleve Key (Classic Drum Museum); **CM** Charlie Morgan; **CW** Charlie Watts; **GNI** Geoff Nicholls; **GNO** Gary Noonan; **JR** Jimmy Ray (Shamrock Drums); **KO** Korg; **LE** Lyn Edwards; **NM** Nick Mason; **NO** Noble & Cooley; **PE** Pearl; **PH** Phillips (London); **SON** Sonor; **SOT** Sotheby's (London); **SW** Steve White; **YA** Yamaha.

KEY TO DRUM PHOTOGRAPHS

The following key is designed to identify who owned which drums when they were photographed for this book. After the relevant page number (*in italic type*) we list: the instrument, followed by the owner's initials in **bold type** (see Owners' Credits above). For example, *'22/23*: Trixon kit **BL**' means that the Trixon kit shown across pages 22 and 23 was owned by Brian Lewis.

Jacket front: Ludwig Super Classic (see below) **BE**. *3*: Pearl kit **PE**. *10/11*: all **AB**. *14/15*: all **AB**. *18/19*: all **AB**. *22*: Trixon snare **BL**. *22/23*: Trixon kit **BL**. *25/26*: Ringo's Premier kit **SOT**. *26*: Olympic snare **GNI**. *27*: Ajax kit **AB**. *28/29*: all **CK**. *32/33*: Ludwig kit **BB**. *33*: Ludwig snare **BB**. *36/37*: Ludwig kit **CC**. *37*: Ludwig pedal **LE**. *40/41*: Gretsch kit **CW**. *44/45*: Keith's White & Copper kit **SOT**. *48*: Hayman snare **LE**. *49*: Ludwig kit **PH**. *50/51*: Hayman kit **AR**. *51*: Carl Palmer's custom kit **SOT**. *54/55*: Pink Floyd Ludwig kit **NM**. *58*: Camco pedal **CM**. *59*: Royal Star snare **CM**. *62/63*: Yamaha kit **YA**. *66*: Noble & Cooley kit **NO**. *69/70*: all **CM**. *72*: Sonor kit **SON**. *76*: Sleishman pedal **JR**; Noonan snare **GNO**. *77*: Mapex kit **KO**. *80/81*: all **SW**. *Jacket back:* Premier snares **CM**.

The Ludwig Super Classic oyster black pearl kit on the front of the jacket consists of a 20" bass drum with 13" and 16" toms (dated 30th September 1965). This kit is the same one that was hired from the musical instrument hire company Beat About The Bush by Apple during the making of *The Beatles Anthology*. The kit is completed by a Supraphonic 400 snare drum belonging to the author, and various Zildjian and Paiste cymbals from the 1960s.

Principal photography was by Miki Slingsby. Other photographs were supplied by the following. Brian Bennett: himself, p22 (both). Bill Bruford: himself, jacket front and p58. Ian Croft: Chad Smith p81. Bob Henrit: himself, p54. Kaman: Moffett p76. Korg: Portnoy p77. Nick Mason: himself, p77. Andy Newmark: himself, p63. Noble & Cooley: Whitten p66; inset drummer p66; Collins p66. Peavey: Rock p76. Simon Phillips: himself, p59. Redfern's: Ulrich jacket front; Chick Webb p15; Krupa/Goodman p18; Starr p33; Appice p36; Pirates p37; Kula Shaker p37; Watts p41; Moon p45 (bottom); Baker p48; Bonham p49; Peart p54; Copeland p58; Hayward p70; Weller p80. Remo UK: Palmer p67; Lawson p67; Bozzio p67. Sonor: Calhoun p71; Thompson p71; Blackman p73; McBrain p73. Yamaha: Bordin p62; Powell p63. Zildjian International: Gadd p63.

Other illustrated items, including catalogues, brochures, magazines, record sleeves, badges and photographs, came from the collections of Arbiter Group, Tony Bacon, Beat About The Bush, Dave Bitelli, Sir Alan Buckley, Decca, Lyn Edwards, Mike Kaskell, *Music Trades* magazine, The National Jazz Archive (Loughton), Geoff Nicholls, Premier and Jimmy Ray. These beautifully conserved items were transformed for your viewing pleasure by Miki Slingsby.

INTERVIEWS

I am grateful to the following, who consented to be interviewed especially for this book: Ivor Arbiter and Johnny Arbiter (Arbiter Group plc); Brian Bennett; Sir Alan Buckley; Clem Cattini; Gerry Evans (Meinl); Bob Henrit; Roy Holliday; Roger Horrobin (Premier Percussion); Andy Newmark; Pat Townsend (Staccato); and Tommy Wilkinson (The London Rock Shop). I've also drawn on previous interviews and conversations (mostly conducted for *Making Music* magazine) with the following: Bill Bruford; Billy Cobham; Lou Dias (Supreme Drums); Ricky Lawson; John Marshall; Dave Mattacks; Nicko McBrain; Gary Noonan; Carl Palmer; Simon Phillips; Pat Picton; Chad Smith; Matt Sorum; Charlie Watts; Alan White; Steve White; Paul Winterhart.

IN ADDITION to those named above in OWNERS' CREDITS and in INTERVIEWS the author and publisher would like to thank: Gwen Alexander; Cliff Bennett; Wayne Blanchard (Sabian); Louis Borenius; Andie Brooke-Mellor (FCN); Mike Brooks (Paiste UK); Martin Cole; Ian Croft (Sonor); Sherry Daly (Charlie Watts); Lou Dias (Supreme Drums); George Frederick (Pearl UK); Darryl Gates (Korg UK); Alan Gilby (Richmo Drums); Kim Graham (Kaman Music Corp); Bill Harrison; Roy Holliday; Carol Jones (Noble & Cooley); Ken Jones (National Jazz Archive, Loughton Library); Michael Kaskell; Chris Lampard (IMP); Brian Majeski (*The Music Trades*); Gary Mann (Remo UK); Jerome Marcus (Sabian); Nick Mason; Dave Mattacks; Ray Minhinnett; Terry Morey (London Industrial plc, Acton Business Centre); Kevin Morris; Jon Newey; Andy Newmark; Sid Phillips; Simon Phillips; Paul Quinn (Making Music); Stephanie Roberts (Pink Floyd); Alan Scally (Korg UK); Martin Scott; Dave Seville (Old Drummers Club); Nick Sharples (Arbiter Group plc); Ian Thomas; Mike U'dell (Drumhire); Harald von Falkenstein (Peavey UK); David 'Clint' Walker; Baz Ward; Bob Wiczling (Zildjian International); Bradley Willatts (Yamaha); Louise Wojnicki (Peavey UK); Joan Woodgate (Startling Music/Ringo Starr).

BIBLIOGRAPHY

John Aldridge *Guide to Vintage Drums* (Centerstream 1994); Brian Ashley & Steve Monnery *Whose Who? A Who Retrospective* (New English Library 1978); Tony Bacon & Paul Day *The Gretsch Book - A Complete History Of Gretsch Electric Guitars* (Balafon/Miller Freeman 1996); James Blades *Percussion Instruments And Their History* (Faber 1984); Michael Braun *Love Me Do! The Beatles Progress* (Penguin 1964); Harry Cangany & Rick Van Horn *The Great American Drums And The Companies That Made Them 1920-1969* (Modern Drummer 1996); Bob Cianci *Great Rock Drummers Of The Sixties* (Hal Leonard 1989); Alan Clayson *Ringo Starr, Straight Man Or Joker?* (Paragon 1991); David Crombie *Piano* (Balafon/IMP 1995); Frank Driggs & Harris Lewine *Black Beauty, White Heat* (Morrow 1982); J Godbolt *History Of Jazz In Britain 1919-1950* (Quartet 1984); Phil Hardy & Dave Laing *The Faber Companion To 20th-Century Popular Music* (Faber 1990); Dezo Hoffmann *With The Beatles: The Historic Photographs Of Dezo Hoffmann* (Omnibus 1982); Barry Kernfeld (ed) *New Grove Dictionary Of Jazz* (Macmillan 1988); Colin Larkin (ed) *The Guinness Encyclopedia Of Popular Music* (Guinness 1992); Mark Lewisohn *The Complete Beatles Chronicle* (Pyramid 1992); Michael Ochs *Rock Archives* (Bath 1984); John Repsch *The Legendary Joe Meek* (Woodford 1989); Herlin Riley & Johnny Vidacovich *New Orleans Jazz And Second Line Drumming* (Manhattan Music 1995); Stanley Sadie (ed) *The New Grove Dictionary of Musical Instruments* (Macmillan 1984); Paul William Schmidt *History Of The Ludwig Drum Company* (Hal Leonard 1991); Schuller, Gunther *Early Jazz* (Oxford University Press 1968); Harry Shapiro *A-Z of Rock Drummers* (Proteus 1982); Ward, Stokes, Tucker *Rock of Ages, The Rolling Stone History of Rock and Roll* (Rolling Stone 1986); Max Weinberg *The Big Beat* (Billboard 1991); Charles White *The Life And Times Of Little Richard* (Pan 1984).

I also consulted and quoted from back issues of the following magazines (in particular *Modern Drummer* and *Rhythm*): *Beat Instrumental; Crescendo; Down Beat; Drums & Drumming; Melody Maker; Modern Drummer; New Musical Express; Not So Modern Drummer; Old Drummers' Club; Rhythm.*

SPECIAL THANKS

While I was writing this book in 1996, Gerry Evans died following a long illness. Gerry was a terrific character and brilliant raconteur, and it was talking with him that convinced me to devote some of this book to the sales and manufacturing background of the 1960s British drum scene. Gerry is greatly missed by his many friends in the British drum business.

Many thanks to Bob Henrit for checking through and commenting on the main text. I take full responsibility for any errors of fact.

Last, a special mention to Lou Dias of Supreme Drums for much encouragement and help over the years.

On the idle hill of summer,
Sleepy with the flow of streams,
Far I hear the steady drummer
Drumming like a noise in dreams.
(A E Housman)

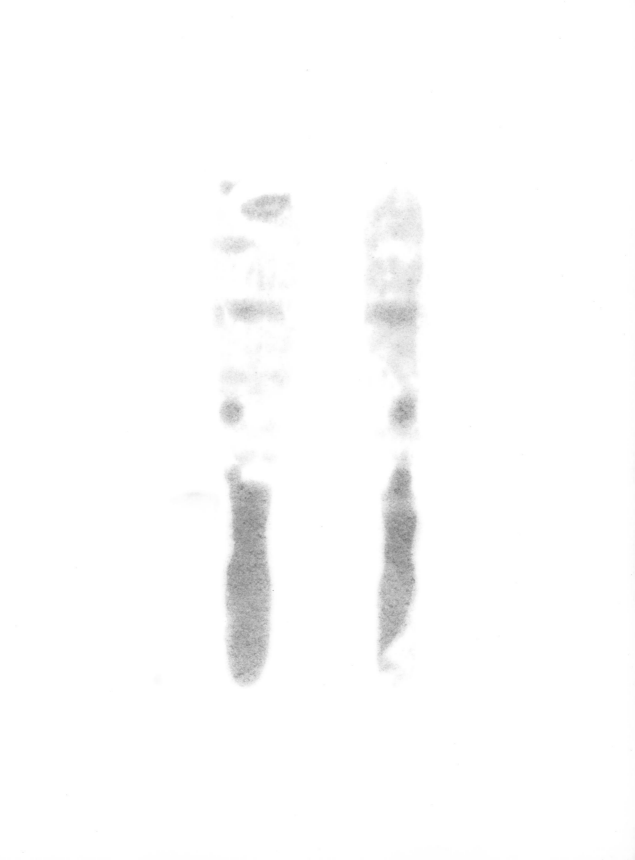

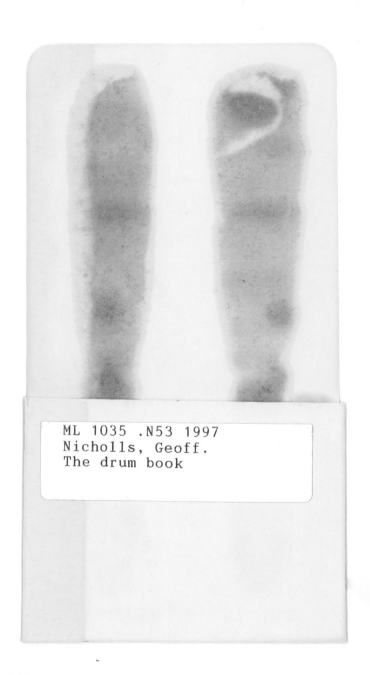